Henry Cooper's Most Memorable Fights

Other books in this series:

Gary Sobers' Most Memorable Matches
Gareth Edwards' Most Memorable Matches
Bobby Charlton's Most Memorable Matches

Henry Cooper's Most Memorable Fights

Henry Cooper
with Norman Giller

Cartoons by
Roy Ullyett

Stanley Paul
London Melbourne Sydney Auckland Johannesburg

This book is dedicated to the memory of
Jim 'The Bishop' Wicks, a champion manager

Stanley Paul & Co. Ltd
An imprint of Century Hutchinson Ltd

17–21 Conway Street, London W1P 6JD

Hutchinson Publishing Group (Australia) Pty Ltd
PO Box 496, Hawthorn, Melbourne, Victoria 3122

Hutchinson Group (NZ) Ltd
PO Box 40–086, Glenfield 10, Auckland

Hutchinson Group (SA) Pty Ltd
PO Box 337, Bergvlei, 2012 South Africa

First published 1985

Phototypeset in Linotron Baskerville by
Input Typesetting Ltd, London

Printed and bound in Great Britain by Anchor Brendon Ltd,
Tiptree, Essex

ISBN 0 09 162700 1

Contents

Acknowledgements

Henry Cooper and Norman Giller wish to thank the compilers of the following publications for reference checks that considerably eased their workload: various volumes of Nat Fleischer's *Ring Record Book and Boxing Encyclopedia*; *Boxing News*, the 'bible' of the fight game; George Whiting's *Great Fights of the Sixties* (Leslie Frewin); Peter Wilson's *Boxing's Greatest Prize* (Stanley Paul), Peter Wilson's *Ringside Seat* (Rich and Cowan); Reg Gutteridge's *The Big Punchers* (Stanley Paul); various editions of *Ring Magazine* and *Boxing Illustrated*; Frank Butler's *A History of Boxing* (Arthur Barker); Nat Fleischer's *The Heavyweight Championship* (Putnam); *Twenty Years* by Freddie Mills (Nicholson & Watson); Harry Carpenter's *A Pictorial History of Boxing* (Collins); *The Greatest* by Muhammad Ali (Hart-Davis MacGibbon); *Sonny Liston, The Champ Nobody Wanted* by A. S. 'Doc' Young (Johnson); Gilbert Odd's *Encyclopedia of Boxing* (Hamlyn).

We would also like to thank Sport & General, Associated Press and Syndication International for the pictures published in this book and Roy Ullyett for proving he has still got a lot of lead left in his pencil. Our thanks, too, to Reg Hayter for pairing Cooper and Giller in a catchweight match, and also to Stanley Paul's Roddy Bloomfield for his expert refereeing.

Seconds Out

I invite you to take a ringside seat with me for a rerun of 20 heavyweight championship fights that all have a special place in my memory scrapbook. Some of them are a bruise on my memory because I was one of the contestants. Others I have seen from the ringside or on closed circuit television, or have studied on film. They are not necessarily the greatest fights that I have seen or taken part in, but all have particular significance, and when you have finished reading the book you will have a complete overall picture of the post-war British and world heavyweight scene. Norman Giller, the writer who has faithfully recorded my views and opinions, has researched the background of every one of the fighters featured in the book, and with a mixture of his facts and my feelings I think we have given a revealing insight into all of the great heavyweight champions and challengers of the past 40 years. Norman usually works in harness with Jimmy Greaves, but I borrowed him so that he could listen to a refined Cockney accent for a change! To light the fuse to endless boxing arguments, my views on the great heavyweight fighters have been matched against the findings of a computer that has rated the world and British champions exclusively for this scrapbook. That is featured as a bonus – a final round – but first come with me to a ringside seat to recapture the drama and excitement of My Most Memorable Fights . . .

Henry Cooper

1
The Fight: Joe Louis v. Jersey Joe Walcott
The Date: 25 June 1948
The Venue: New York Yankee Stadium

The Build-up

Like most sportsdaft kids growing up in the immediate post-war years I idolized Joe Louis. He was the first fighter to capture my imagination and fuel my dreams of one day becoming a champion of the ring. His world title defence against Jersey Joe Walcott had special significance because it was widely publicized as being his swansong. Win or lose, Louis planned to retire and bring down the curtain on a career that had lifted him into the realm of legend. The fact that his retirement plan was torpedoed by the taxman is one of the saddest stories in sport.

No book about heavyweight championship boxing would be complete without a tribute to the great Louis. To leave him out would be like writing about great composers and not mentioning Bach or Beethoven . . . or penning a history of the most influential writers without reference to Shakespeare or Dickens. I make no excuse for waxing lyrical about Louis.

He was a master of boxing and nobody can exaggerate his standing in the sport.

At his peak, Joe took on and beat all-comers. They called it his 'bum of the month' campaign when he was bowling over challengers for his championship at intervals of just a few weeks. It wasn't that his opponents were so bad as that Louis was in a class of his own.

Nobody could have had a more humble start in life than Joe, who was born Joseph Louis Barrow in a ramshackle cabin in the cotton fields of Lexington, Alabama. The seventh child of Monroe and Lily Barrow, he was of Cherokee Indian, Negro-white stock and he grew up in abject poverty. When he was ten his family moved to Detroit and Joe started playing truant from violin lessons to study boxing at a local gymnasium. He certainly never fiddled around in the ring and when he was 19 won the coveted US Golden Gloves light-heavyweight title before launching his professional career in July 1934.

His one and only defeat in his first 14 years as a professional was a stunning 12th-round knockout by Germany's former world champion Max Schmeling in his 22nd fight, on 19 June 1936. Louis took the world title from James J. Braddock with an eighth-round knockout victory a year and three days later and then, in one of his toughest defences, outpointed Welsh lionheart Tommy Farr. A year to the day after winning the championship he savagely avenged his one defeat by stopping Schmeling in just 124 seconds of a sensational fight that whipped up ugly anti-Nazi feelings.

Louis was still champion ten years later after 24 successful defences, 21 of his victories having been completed inside the distance. He had won all but one of his 60 professional fights and among his impressive list of victims were former world champions Primo Carnera, Max Baer, Jack Sharkey, Braddock and, of course, Schmeling. I have selected his second fight with Jersey Joe Walcott for inclusion in my Most

Memorable Fights scrapbook because it grabbed my attention
when I was at an impressionable age.

We, that's my twin brother George and I, were 15 years
old at the time of the second Louis-Walcott contest and were
just starting out on the boxing ladder with the Eltham and
District Amateur Boxing Club. We were both locked in to
the legend that was Louis.

My infatuation was so deep rooted that I used to stand in
front of the mirror at home in Bellingham and pretend I was
Louis throwing his famed and feared left hook. The fact that
I was a skinny nine stone and dough white while Louis was
a muscular 6 ft. 1½ in. and just a couple of shades off being
as black as the ace of spades will prove that, if nothing else,
I was a kid with a vivid imagination. It was no co-incidence
that it was the left hook that later became the most destructive
weapon in my armoury. George and I strongly identified with
Louis because he represented all that was best about the fight
game. He was dignified and sporting as well as being a genius
of a ring craftsman with brilliant boxing ability; and he
carried a knockout punch in either fist that was said to be like
a bomb landing. That's why he was nicknamed the 'Brown
Bomber'.

A lot of the kids with whom we went to school were into
tuppenny comic heroes like Rockfist Rogan of the *Champion*
and the multi-talented Wilson of the *Wizard*. But not George
and I. We liked our heroes to be flesh and blood, not made of
paper. There was Denis Compton, of Arsenal and Middlesex.
Stanley Matthews, the wizard of dribble. Sydney Wooderson,
the tiny, galloping, bespectacled solicitor who was a miling
master. And, biggest of all in our personal hall of fame, stood
the king of the ring Joe Louis.

To our young eyes, Jersey Joe Walcott was the villain
standing in the way of an invincible hero, and in our fertile
imaginations we sketched out a battle plan in which Louis
would attack from the opening bell and land a succession of
the murderous short hooks that were his speciality. These

power-propelled punches would bring him a first-round knockout victory for a fitting finale to his career. A pity we forgot to show the script to Jersey Joe Walcott.

We had the right needle with Walcott because just six months earlier he had taken Louis to a 15–round points decision in a title fight at the old Madison Square Garden. There was a bigger stink than you used to get in Billingsgate Fish Market when two judges voted for the champion to ensure that Louis kept hold of the world crown. That greatly respected referee Ruby Goldstein reckoned, like most ringside spectators, that Walcott had done more than enough to win the fight but he was outvoted two-to-one. For my brother George and me the only thing that mattered was that Louis was still the king and we were convinced he would leave no room for argument in the return fight in the New York Yankee Stadium.

What we didn't really appreciate at the time was that Walcott himself was one hell of a fighter. He had borrowed the name Joe Walcott from a famous welterweight boxer who had been world champion at the turn of the century. Joe's real name was Arnold Cream. With a name like that he had to be handy with his fists. Blimey, if we'd have owned up to being called that when we were growing up on London's south side of the Thames we'd have had more fights outside the ring than we ever had inside the ropes.

Walcott, at 34 just four months older than the champion, had been around as a professional four years longer than Louis but without getting anything like the acclaim and admiration that had made the Brown Bomber a world-wide idol. He had lied about his age so that he could launch his professional career at barely 15 and he had been swindled so many times by unscrupulous managers and promoters that he kept giving up boxing in disgust.

Walcott, a God-fearing man who always carried a Bible with him outside the ring, was a hungry fighter in the truest sense. He had a wife and six children to feed and continually had to answer the call of the ring to make ends meet. His hungriest years were between 1938 and 1945 when he had just seven fights and went on the dole to pay the food bills.

One freezing cold evening in the winter of 1945 Walcott was visited at his Jersey home by a boxing manager called Felix Bocchicchio, who wanted Jersey Joe to sign with him. Walcott pointed to an empty coalbin in the corner of his living room and said: 'Mister, if you can keep that bin full for me I will fight for you.' Over the next eight years under Bocchicchio's shrewd management Walcott earned enough to buy a coalmine.

In their first two years together Jersey Joe fought 21 times, losing just three and avenging each defeat. His victims included top-class fighters of the calibre of Joe Baksi, Lee Oma and Joey Maxim. He was a crafty and shifty box-fighter, bewildering opponents with clever footwork and feints, and he had the punching power to finish fights with one well-executed blow.

After joining up with the silver-tongued Bocchicchio he took part in eight world title fights including two with Louis. The hungry years were over. Jersey Joe Walcott had come in from the cold.

All of this, of course, meant nothing to the Cooper twins down in south-east London. As far as we were concerned there was only one man who mattered in the world heavyweight championship fight at the Yankee Stadium, New York, in 1948 – and that was our hero Joe Louis.

The Fight

I have been able to study film of the second Louis–Walcott fight and, to be honest, for most of the time it was a stinker. Louis was heavy footed and fought like a man who has had two or three fights too many. Walcott, 20 pounds lighter at

13 st. 12 lb. and, at 6 ft., an inch-and-a-half shorter than the champion, was the more mobile and moved about the ring on slim, strong legs that were like those of a dancer rather than a ring-worn fighter.

Louis kept reaching down into his memory to try to recall the precision and power of his peak years, but for most of the fight he was a shambling shadow of himself. He resorted to uncharacteristic spoiling tactics and both champion and challenger were continually tangled up in the centre of the ring. In fact there were more clinches than in a Joan Collins film.

Walcott dropped Louis for a short count in the third and would have been ahead on the scorecards of even the most biased judges as the untidy championship contest moved laboriously into the last third of its scheduled 15 rounds. Then suddenly in the 11th round Louis, as if touched by a magic wand, found the form and the fire that had deserted him.

He backed Walcott onto the ropes and turned his dancing tormentor into a statue with a right cross that would have finished the fight there and then had the ropes not held the challenger up. In the blinking of an eye Louis unleashed a salvo of ten punches to the head, wicked hooks and crosses that carried the rhythmic timing and explosive power of a born fighter.

I have rarely seen punches thrown with such blinding speed. They were almost a blur and I had to scrutinize the film in slow motion for confirmation that, including the first pole-axeing right, 11 punches thudded through Walcott's devastated defence. He sank slowly to the canvas like a stricken ship going down at sea and the ten-second count was a mere formality.

It was hours later when two ecstatic Cooper brothers tuned into the old Light programme on the wireless and heard the news of how Louis had retained the world championship with an 11th-round knock-out victory. The fact that he and

14

Walcott had managed to send spectators almost numb with boredom before the electrifying finish didn't bother George and me. Our hero had won. Joe Louis was still the King.

The Aftermath:

Louis cemented himself even deeper into our hearts when he announced after his victory: 'That one was for my Mom. Now I'm gonna hang up my gloves. I will never fight again.' But, sadly, there was an opponent waiting around the corner that Louis could never beat – the taxman.

During his career there were times when so many people were dipping into his pocket that he was sometimes having to pay out 110 per cent of his purse money to hangers-on. The one unsolicited partner he did not pay was the Inland Revenue and they floored him after the second Walcott fight with a thumping tax demand. Poor old Joe had to pull the gloves on again and two years later he was painfully outpointed by Ezzard Charles, a fighter he would have licked in his prime. Charles then lost the championship to Jersey Joe who, at 37, became the oldest boxer ever to win the world heavyweight crown.

The fight with Charles was the Brown Bomber's 27th and last for the world championship and the only one in which he finished a loser. Twenty-three of his 26 victories came inside the distance. Only Tommy Farr, Arturo Godoy and Walcott stayed the full course with him and both Godoy and Walcott were knocked out in return fights.

Louis continued to be hounded by the taxman and, after a run of eight undistinguished wins, was matched with a young unbeaten white heavyweight called Rocky Marciano. Their non-title fight finished in the eighth round with the battered Louis lying stretched through the ropes, his balding head on the ring apron and his legs spreadeagled on the canvas. Referee Ruby Goldstein spared Joe the indignity of being counted out and stopped the one-sided contest. It was Joe's last fight.

He had won 68 of his 71 contests but, much more than that, he had won the hearts of millions of people around the world who respected his skill and admired his conduct in and out of the ring. When Louis died in Las Vegas in 1981 a month short of his 67th birthday, the world mourned the passing of one of the greatest and most popular sportsmen of the century. He will remain a hero for all time in the eyes of the twin brothers from Bellingham who built their dreams of boxing fame on a foundation laid by the one and only Joe Louis.

As far as George and I are concerned, the legend of Louis lives on.

For the Record:

Joe Louis

Born Lexington, Alabama, 13 May 1914.
Ht.: 6 ft. 1½ in. Wt.: 14 st. 6 lb.
Turned professional in 1934 after winning the US amateur light-heavyweight title. Managed by Julian Black and John Roxborough, and later Marshall Miles.
Honours: world heavyweight champion, 1937–49. Successfully defended the world title a record 25 times.
Record: 71 fights, 68 wins, 3 losses (1 KO); 55 inside-the-distance wins (43 KOs).

Jersey Joe Walcott

Born Merchantville, New Jersey.
Ht.: 6 ft. Wt.: 13 st. 12 lb.
Turned professional at 15. Managed in his prime by Felix Bocchicchio.

Honours: world heavyweight champion 1951–2. At 37, the oldest man ever to win the title.

Record: 67 fights, 49 wins, 1 draw, 17 losses (6 KOs); 31 inside-the-distance wins (29 KOs).

2

The Fight: Bruce Woodcock v. Freddie Mills
The Date: 2 June 1949
The Venue: White City Stadium, London

The Build-up

British boxing was on its knees immediately after the Second
World War and only the flair of showman promoter Jack
Solomons and the fire of Bruce Woodcock and Freddie Mills
saved the fight game from being counted out. There was so
little crowd-drawing talent in our rings that there would have
been no major promotions in London if these three had not
been around.

Solomons, unchallenged in the 1940s and 1950s as the self-
styled king of promoters, staged a series of shows featuring
Woodcock and Mills against imported opponents. I'm not so
sure this over-exposure was healthy for either boxer because
it seemed to me that both of them were too often pushed out
of their depth in the sole interest of box-office business.

Woodcock, born in Doncaster on 18 January 1921, suffered
by being rushed to the top before he had finished his boxing
apprenticeship. He turned professional in 1942, three years
after winning the ABA light-heavyweight title that was to

come into my custody some 13 years later. He captured the British and Empire heavyweight championships in his 21st fight by knocking out old-stager Jack London in the sixth round at Tottenham's football ground at White Hart Lane in 1945.

Over the next six months Woodcock stretched his unbeaten run to 25 professional contests and proved beyond question that he was one of the few potential world-class heavyweights Britain has produced. But most of his victories were gained against mediocre opposition, and while he was waiting to go through with a non-title fight against Freddie Mills in 1946 his handlers stupidly sent him to New York for a ten-round fight against a guy called Tami Mauriello, who was one of the roughest, toughest customers ever to climb through the ropes.

For Woodcock it was like leaving a goldfish bowl and jumping into a tankful of piranha fish. His good old English left jab, his hard but conventional right cross and his obedience to the gentlemanly rules of boxing as laid down by the Marquess of Queensberry left him easy prey for Mauriello, a world-ranked veteran of 80 fights who was more accustomed to the law of the jungle.

Mauriello was getting the worst of it against Woodcock's superior boxing skills but soon cancelled out this minor irritation by blatantly butting the Yorkshireman right between the eyes. Woodcock was still dazed when the brawling Italian-American sent over a clubbing right in the fifth round that flattened him for the full ten-second count. Incidentally, on going through Mauriello's ring record I noticed that he twice knocked out a geezer who rejoiced in the name of Henry Cooper. I promise it wasn't me. I was still a young amateur and in awe of the likes of Woodcock and Freddie Mills.

Anyway, just three weeks later Woodcock went ahead with his non-title fight against Mills who was himself trying to recover after a tenth-round defeat by Gus Lesnevich in a bloody and violent battle for the world light-heavyweight championship in London on 14 May 1946. Mills had been decked four times in the second round, but with the courage that was to become his trademark he clawed his way back into the fight only to run into more double-fisted trouble in the tenth round when the referee came to his rescue after he had taken two more counts.

It would have been sensible if both Woodcock and Mills had taken at least a couple of months off after their painful defeats but, like I say, the box office came first and Jack Solomons had a packed house waiting for them at Harringay Arena on 4 June 1946. They knocked hell out of each other for 12 rounds before Woodcock, with both eyes nearly closed, had his hand raised as a points winner.

I doubt if there has ever been a braver fighter than Freddie Mills. In fact he was too brave for his own good. He learned his craft in the hardest school of all, the fairground boxing booths in which he would sometimes have more than half a dozen scraps in one evening. He used to take on all-comers and it was nothing for him to climb into the ring dwarfed by opponents two or three stone heavier. He didn't know the meaning of the word fear.

Mills, born in Bournemouth on 26 June 1919, idolized Jack Dempsey when he was a kid and there was certainly some similiarity in his fighting style, although he lacked the Manassa Mauler's crushing knock-out punch.

While boxing in the booths he teamed up with a wily old Welsh professional called Gipsy Daniels, a former British light-heavyweight champion who in his peak year of 1928 had gone to Germany and knocked out Max Schmeling in the first round. He was on the downhill run when he met up with Mills but he passed on invaluable tricks of the trade during hundreds of rounds of sparring.

It meant Mills was already a seasoned campaigner when he officially launched his professional career after winning a novice competition in Bournemouth in 1936. He squashed 72 fights into his first five and a half years as a professional and

then sensationally established himself in the top flight by stopping the great middleweight favourite Jock McAvoy in one round. Freddie followed this up by knocking out ageing Len Harvey in two rounds in 1942 to win the British and Empire light-heavyweight titles.

Once he had finished wartime service in the RAF, Mills continually agreed to take on opponents bigger and, frankly, better than himself, counting on his giant heart and all-out aggressive style of fighting to get him through. 'Fearless Freddie' was a formidable light-heavyweight but he was too often tempted to step up into the heavyweight division where he had neither the physique nor the punching power to make his presence felt. In November 1946, he unwisely agreed to fight giant Czech-American Joe Baksi on a Jack Solomons promotion at Earls Court. Baksi had a jutting jaw like Desperate Dan and punches in either hand that could have been measured on the Richter scale. There was no way Mills could give more than two stone away to a fighter of Baksi's class and he was hammered to a sixth-round defeat.

Sitting ringside that night was Woodcock and his advisers. Solomons offered them Baksi as an opponent and, instead of reacting as if they were within touching distance of a plague, they nodded their heads and accepted one of the silliest matches in British boxing history. Baksi broke Woodcock's jaw in the first round with a mighty left hook and the gutsy man from Doncaster was finally rescued by the referee in the seventh after collecting injuries that put him in hospital and on the sidelines for 18 months. Baksi made such a great impact that his name lives on even today in Cockney rhyming slang. If you ever hear a Londoner saying 'Call me a Joe', it means a Joe Baksi – taxi. Here endeth the Cockney rabbit lesson.

Anyway, while Woodcock was out of action Freddie Mills became the hero of British sport by taking the world light-heavyweight crown from Gus Lesnevich, winning on points over 15 rounds in a fierce, thrilling battle at Harringay Arena on 26 July 1948. Soon afterwards Jack Solomons decided that the stage was set for a return with Woodcock, and the following June the two men sized up to each other at the White City.

The Fight

Woodcock, a nicely built heavyweight at 6 ft. ½ in. and nearly 14 st., had a 20 lb weight advantage over the giant-hearted Mills, but it was Mills who was a slight favourite with the bookies because of his new status of world champion. Woodcock's three titles – British, European and Empire – were on the line and the White City Stadium was sold out, which meant Solomons was able to pay both fighters a then record purse of £14,000 each. That must have been the equivalent of about a hundred grand each by today's values. It was good money but, blimey, they had to earn every penny.

Mills took the fight to Woodcock from the first bell, swinging wildly with both hands in a bid to knock the smooth-moving Yorkshireman out of his stride. But Woodcock remained cool and calm and kept sticking out his long, solid left jab. Just before the bell to end the first round Woodcock unleashed a straight right to the side of the head followed by a right cross to the jaw. Mills fell to his knees but hauled himself up before a count could start. The bell saved him from a follow-up attack.

Studying the fight on film, it looks a mismatch. Mills was so clearly outgunned, yet because of his game spirit and busy, two-fisted attacks he was always keeping himself in the fight, and the way Woodcock's nose was streaming blood from the fourth round is evidence that he was not having things completely his own way. The major difference between them was the power of their punches. Mills was landing some full-blooded blows that had little effect on Woodcock, whereas Woodcock wobbled the world light-heavyweight champion almost every time he connected with his favourite right crosses and hooks.

Mills took short counts in the third and eighth rounds and a left-right combination to the head dropped him for nine in the tenth. A brave heart can carry you only so far and Freddie finally had to succumb to Woodcock's heavier artillery. He was boxing in a daze from the tenth round and the inevitable finish came in the 14th when Woodcock was bang on target with a left hook and right cross to the side of the jaw. Mills was counted out on his knees. A good little 'un had bowed to a good big 'un.

The Aftermath

The victory re-established Woodcock as Britain's top box-office draw and Solomons shrewdly steered him into a match with American Lee Savold that was billed as being for the world heavyweight championship following the retirement of Joe Louis. The fight was postponed until 6 June 1950, because Woodcock damaged his shoulder in a crash after falling asleep at the wheel of a truck.

There was a crowd of more than 50,000 fans shoe-horned into the White City Stadium for a fight that was recognized as a championship contest only in Britain. Woodcock started well, shaking Savold with his mighty right. But his wars with Mills and the shellacking he had taken from Baksi had caught up with him and he was forced to retire at the end of four rounds with a jagged cut over his right eye.

Had today's strict British Boxing Board of Control medical checks been in operation, it's unlikely that Bruce would ever have been allowed to fight again. He has since admitted that he defied medical advice about the dangers of permanent damage to his eyes and went through with one more contest. He surrendered his British and Empire titles to giant ex-guardsman Jack Gardner after 11 punishing rounds at Earls Court on 14 November 1950.

Freddie Mills was so ring-worn that he could manage only one more fight. He defended his world light-heavyweight championship against American Joey Maxim at Earls Court on 24 January 1950, and all those hard battles of the previous five years weighed heavily on him as Maxim handed him a mummy and a daddy of a hiding. He was knocked out in the tenth round after a fusillade of punches had ripped three teeth out of his gums. A few months later happy-go-lucky Mills managed to cash in on this unsolicited dental work with a popular record called 'All I Want for Christmas is Me Two Front Teeth'.

The fight against Maxim was Freddie's last stand. He retired from the ring and invested what was left of the record £80,000 he had earned during his career in a restaurant, a night-club and boxing promotions. Freddie had a lovely personality and was always full of wisecracks and laughter that kept him in demand as a television and radio personality.

But there was sadness hidden behind the laughter and few people knew the personal problems he had. His tragic and mysterious death from a gunshot wound in 1965 shocked and saddened his army of admirers. It was described as a suicide but those of us who knew him well just couldn't accept that Freddie would ever throw the towel in. I was a big fan of his and will always remember him for his extraordinary courage. They don't come braver than Fearless Freddie Mills.

For the Record

Bruce Woodcock

Born Doncaster, 18 January 1921.
Ht.: 6 ft. ½ in. Wt.: 13 st. 12 lb.
ABA light-heavyweight champion 1939.
Turned professional 1942. Manager: Tom Hurst.

Honours: British, European and Empire heavyweight titles.
Record: 38 fights, 34 wins, 4 losses (1 KO); 32 inside-the-distance
wins (10 KOs).

Freddie Mills

Born Bournemouth, June 26, 1919.
Ht.: 5 ft. 10 in. Wt.: 12 st. 6 lb.
Won a novices competition at the age of 16. Turned professional
1936. Manager: Ted Broadribb.
Honours: world, British, European and Empire light-heavyweight
titles.
Record: 96 fights, 73 wins, 6 draws, 17 losses (4 KOs); 52 inside-
the-distance wins (26 KOs).

3

The Fight: Rocky Marciano v. Don Cockell
The Date: 16 May 1955
The Venue: Kezar Stadium, San Francisco

The Build-up

My professional career was just eight months and eight fights old when Don Cockell, then the British and Empire heavyweight champion, accepted the chance we all dream about: a crack at the world title. It was just poor old Don's luck that the championship happened to be in the keeping of the most vicious and violent champion in ring history, Rocky Marciano.

Cockell was a former blacksmith born and brought up only a training run away from me along the Thames south embankment at Battersea. As a fellow South Londoner I was naturally right behind him in his bid for the title, but my private feelings were: 'Rather you than me, mate.' I've often offered up a silent prayer of thanks that Marciano wasn't around when I was at my peak. I think I would have fancied going into a cage with a lion rather than into the ring with Rocky, who used his fists like sledgehammers and showed little or no respect for the rules of boxing. He was so crude

27

and primitive in the way he launched his attacks that they called him the Twentieth-Century Caveman, but nobody could deny that the end result was sensational. At the finish of his fights his opponents used to look as if they had been victims of car crashes.

Marciano's rise to fame and fortune was like something out of a Hollywood movie. Come to think of it, they could have called his lifestory Rocky! He was born Rocco Marchegiano in Brockton, Massachusetts, the eldest of six children of immigrant Italian parents. I've got a lovely Italian wife, Albina, and so I have taken a closer than usual interest in Rocky's background. His father, Pirrino, emigrated to the United States from the tiny fishing village of Chieti on the Adriatic coast. His mother, Pasqualena, was from San Bartolomeo, near Naples. Pirrino returned to Europe with the US army six years before Rocky was born and was so badly gassed during a First World War battle that he was rarely able to hold down a full-time job as a cobbler. So Rocky, who weighed in on 1 September 1923, grew up in a tough environment that helped shape him into the mean, merciless man who was to later dominate the world heavyweight scene.

Rocky concentrated on American football and baseball at school and it wasn't until he was called up by the US army that he started to take a serious interest in boxing. He had one of his first scraps *outside* the ring in the unlikely setting of a South Wales pub. Rocky, who had been on duty loading supplies ready for the 1944 Normandy Invasion, was 'volunteered' by his mates to uphold the honour of the United States after a large, drunken Australian had started dishing out some no-holds-barred verbal insults. Legend has it that Rocky silenced the Aussie with a swift left down under and a right to the head that knocked the wind out of him and provided a preview of what was in store for a procession of professional opponents. He never did lose that bar-room brawler image.

When the war was over, Rocky fought briefly as an amateur

and then hitch-hiked from Brockton to New York for a gymnasium trial under the all-knowing gaze of Madison Square Garden matchmaker Al Weill. Most onlookers didn't know whether to laugh or cry when they saw Marciano's pathetic attempts at sparring. He was as clumsy on his feet as a cross-legged calf and his defence was non-existent. But Weill noted Rocky's raw power and had the vision to realize that he could be moulded into a fearsome force. He put him under the wing of veteran English-born trainer Charley Goldman, an old-time bantamweight who knew every boxing trick in the book and quite a few that never quite got into print.

Goldman, a chirpy character who always had a bowler hat jammed on his head, got to work on Rocky behind closed doors. He first of all set about getting his balance right, roping his legs together so that he was forced out of the habit of adopting too wide a stance. Then he did his best to help Rocky build a defence, concentrating on getting him to bob, weave and turn from the waist so that he could pivot and have full leverage for his punches. Next he showed him how to throw a left jab and following right. The rest Charley left to nature. He knew that Rocky was an instinctive swinger and he was careful not to overcoach him and so risk lessening his natural power and strength. He didn't make the mistake, as so many coaches do, of turning a naturally gifted sportsman into a brain-washed robot.

At 5 ft. 10 ½ in. and 13 st. 2 lb., Rocky did not have the ideal build and his reach at 68 inches was the shortest of any world heavyweight champion. His fists measured just 11½ in. (only Jack Dempsey and Gene Tunney were smaller, both at 11¼ in. – Sonny Liston's were the biggest at 15 in.). But the tale of the tape doesn't give the overall picture of a man who simply oozed menace. Neither does it record that Rocky had the physical strength of a weightlifter and a tough jaw that could withstand the hardest punches. He was a great believer in leg strength and spent hours on the run, building

29

stamina and durability. I doubt if there has ever been a fitter fighting machine. Certainly no champion before or since has sacrificed so much of his time to hermit-like training routines.

Rocky started out as he meant to carry on in his professional debut on St Patrick's Day 1947. He knocked out Lee Epperson in the third round at Holyoke. They then tucked him away for a year while Charley Goldman smoothed some of the rough edges. By the end of 1948 he'd had 11 more fights and his opponents had lasted a total of 15 rounds! Eight of his victories were first-round knock-outs. Al Weill was picking Marciano's opponents with shrewd care, but even if he was going into the ring with dummies it still took a certain quality to win in such whirlwind fashion. Rocky's quality was sheer, raw, earthquaking power.

By 1951 he had stretched his unbeaten run to 35 bouts totalling only 146 rounds and had picked up the nickname the Brockton Blockbuster. It was an impressive record that earned him a make-or-break battle with another fast-rising 'white hope', Rex Layne.

Marciano blasted Layne to a knock-out defeat in six rounds and then polished off highly rated Freddy Beshore in four to set up an intriguing match with my idol, Joe Louis. It's sad history that the old Brown Bomber was grounded in the eighth round of what proved to be his last fight.

Rocky ripped the world championship away from Jersey Joe Walcott in his 43rd fight on 23 September 1952, coming from behind to knock out the old champion in the 13th round with a swinging right that Charley Goldman called his 'Suzy Q' punch. In a return match Suzy landed on Walcott's jaw in the first round and it was all over in 2 minutes 25 seconds. Then the murderous Marciano disposed of Roland LaStarza with a savage assault that forced the referee's intervention in the 11th round. He made two successful defences against former champion Ezzard Charles in 1954, winning on points the first time and scoring an eighth-round knock-out in the return, but at the price of an appalling gash on his nose. It took a long time for the cut to heal and when he was ready to fight again eight months later they looked to Britain for his next challenger in the considerable shape of Don Cockell.

The American Press gave Don shameful treatment in the build-up to the fight. They dismissed him as 'a fat bum' who could not fight. Their conclusions were based on a fourth-round defeat in 1952 by New Yorker Jimmy Slade which was followed by an 11th-round stoppage by Randolph Turpin when Don was shorn of his British, European and Empire light-heavyweight titles.

What the Yanks didn't know – perhaps didn't want to know – is that when Don went through with those fights he was desperately weakened by a glandular problem that meant he was having to spend hours in the Turkish baths shedding unwanted pounds. Hardly the way to prepare for a fight, particularly against top-quality opponents like Slade and Turpin.

When Don appeared in the ring four months after the Turpin defeat he had ballooned to an almost unrecognizable 14 st. 10 lb. But all the skill that had helped make him one of the world's leading light-heavyweights was still there and he was still as light on his feet and as quick with his jolting left jab as when he first turned professional at the age of 17 back in 1946.

In his third fight as a heavyweight he stopped veteran Tommy Farr in seven rounds to set up a British and Empire title fight with Johnny Williams, a fast and clever boxer who was outmanoeuvred over 15 rounds by the tubby but highly mobile Cockell. He then launched into a series of impressive victories against international opposition, including a ten-round points win against Italian Uber Bacilieri who was to be my first overseas opponent two years later. He retained his Empire crown with a points victory over Johnny Arthur in Johannesburg, outscored former world title challenger Roland LaStarza in London and achieved three convincing victories over highly regarded American heavyweight Harry 'Kid'

Matthews. His third success against Matthews in the American's home territory of Seattle convinced Al Weill that Don was a suitable challenger for the world championship.

The Fight

There's a Tony Bennett song called 'I Left My Heart in San Francisco'. Don Cockell had his heart broken there after giving one of the bravest displays of defiance ever seen in any championship fight.

Everything was loaded against Cockell. He had been assured that the fight would be staged in a 20 ft. ring but had a 16½ ft. square ring swung on him when it was too late to mount more than a token protest. Marciano was a hunter of a fighter who liked to hound his opponents to the ropes where he would unleash his heaviest blows. The smaller the ring, the quicker he could trap them. For a light-footed boxer like Cockell, it was akin to having to fight in a telephone kiosk. There was no place to hide.

Also against Cockell was the size of the gloves, changed from six-ounce to eight-ounce to reduce the chances of Marciano's scarred nose being cut again. Before he climbed into the ring, Don told manager John Simpson: 'No matter what happens in there I don't want you stopping it. I want to leave the ring with my head held high.'

This was said privately to Simpson, not for publicity purposes. Don was one of the proudest people I have ever known and there was no way he was going to let Britain or himself down. He put up such a stubborn, gutsy display that Marciano had to resort to gutter tactics to get the better of him. If the fight had been staged outside the United States, where there was a no-foul rule in operation, there is no doubt that Rocky would have been disqualified.

Cockell was continually butted, elbowed and hit below the belt; and he was three times shaken by blows thrown after

32

the bell. The referee allowed Marciano to get away with murder and didn't once warn him for a procession of fouls that would have led to him being thrown out of most rings.

The champion had been kept on the end of the challenger's stabbing left hand for the first two rounds, but from the third Marciano started to find his range with haymakers as he bullied his way through Don's defence. Midway through the fourth round there was a sickening crash of heads as Marciano came boring in like a crazed bull. Cockell reeled back with blood pouring from a two-inch gash on his forehead. Don told me years later that it was the turning point of the fight. 'I was out on my feet and only instinct kept me up,' he said. 'From then on Marciano was just a blur because I couldn't see properly.'

For the next four rounds Cockell shifted some terrible punishment but took it all without complaint, including a barrage of punches after the bell and at least five blows that sunk in below the belt. As his strength drained out of him, Cockell abandoned his hit-and-hop-it tactics and tried to stand toe to toe and slug it out. That was like attempting to take on the fastest gun in the West with a water pistol.

He was completely outgunned and in the ninth round collapsed to the canvas under a swarming two-fisted attack that included a shattering right to the jaw while he was on one knee. The crowd cheered his blind courage as he hauled himself up at nine and the referee mercifully came to the rescue as Marciano pounded him against the ropes.

The Aftermath

Medals have been awarded to men showing less gallantry than Cockell displayed against Marciano. But all he had to show for his crazy bravery was a fair pay day and the admiration of everybody who witnessed his astonishing stand. What didn't show until some time later were the effects of the hammering that he took. Don was never the same man again and after inside-the-distance defeats by giant Cuban Nino Valdes and then Tongan Kitione Lave he announced his retirement. His health suffered and it was a sad day when he finally gave in to a long illness and died on 17 July 1983. He was 54.

I never once heard him complain about the diabolical treatment he received in the States. 'I went in with my eyes open,' he said. 'Marciano knew only one way to fight and I was hoping I could use my superior boxing skill to stay out of trouble. But that feller would have punched his way through a wall.'

Marciano was disbelieving when British sportswriters asked him why he had adopted such roughhouse tactics against Cockell. He had no idea where half his punches were landing. His fouling was not premeditated. He just used to swing and give it everything he had.

He made one more title defence, against Archie Moore on 21 September 1951, knocking 'Ageless Archie' out in the ninth round after he had himself been dropped early in the fight for only the second time in his career. Rocky then became the first heavyweight champion to hang up his gloves with an unblemished record – 49 fights, 49 wins. (Gene Tunney retired while undefeated champion, but had suffered a points set-back earlier in his career against Harry Grebb.)

There was an offer of a million dollars for Marciano to come out of retirement to fight his successor Floyd Patterson, but he was happy with the four million he had made during his career (much of it allegedly buried away in sealed tins!). Rocky was a devoted family man and felt he had sacrificed enough time away from his loved ones in his lonely, punishing hours of training.

I was privileged to get to know him after his retirement and was never able to associate the gentle, quietly spoken, modest man that I met in London with the butcher who had terrorized and tamed the world's greatest heavyweights.

Rocky did have one more fight of sorts. He and Muhammad Ali faked their way through a computerized battle in 1969 in which they simulated seven different finishes. Just two weeks before the film was released – with Marciano winning by a tenth-round knock-out – Rocky was killed when a private plane in which he was a passenger crashed in Iowa. He died on 31 August 1969 – the day before his 46th birthday.

It was my great honour to read the lesson at a requiem mass at the Italian Church in Hatton Garden. Among the church ushers was Don Cockell.

Rocky Marciano and Don Cockell. We won't see their like again.

For the Record

Rocky Marciano

Born Brockton, Mass., 1 September 1923.
Ht.: 5 ft. 10½ in. Wt.: 13 st. 2 lb.
Turned professional 1947. Manager: Al Weill.
Honours: undefeated world heavyweight champion, 1952–5.
Record: 49 fights, 49 wins; 43 inside-the-distance wins (32 KOs).

Don Cockell

Born Battersea, 22 September 1928.
Ht.: 5 ft. 10 in. Wt.: 15 st.
Turned professional aged 17 in 1946. Manager: John Simpson.
Honours: British, European and Empire light-heavyweight titles; British and Empire heavyweight titles.
Record: 79 fights, 64 wins, 1 draw, 14 losses (3 KOs); 36 inside-the-distance wins (19 KOs).

4

The Fight: Henry Cooper v. Brian London
The Date: 12 January 1959
The Venue: Earls Court, London

The Build-up

Brian London created a little bit of history when he bowled
Joe Erskine over in eight rounds to win the British and Empire
heavyweight titles on 3 June 1958. It completed a unique
father-and-son double because 14 years earlier his dad, Jack
London, had outpointed Freddie Mills for the vacant British
heavyweight title.

I was delighted with London's victory but only for selfish
reasons. In the fight game you know deep down when you're
somebody's guv'nor and I was confident I would always have
his measure. It was not the same in Joe Erskine's case, and
so I was pleased that London had taken over as champion
because it meant my chance had to come. And a good chance,
at that.

The Londons and the Coopers had been entwined in a sort
of family feud for some time. I beat his brother, Jack, as an
amateur. Brian evened things up by stopping my brother,
George, in four rounds on 17 January 1956.

As he was from Blackpool, the media built up a North v. South rivalry between us and it became like the Ewings v. the Barnes family. I'd have to say Brian was the JR of the scenario because he could be a nasty bit of work in and out of the ring.

He used to scowl and give off bad vibrations at weigh-ins and press conferences, and in the ring he was, frankly, a bit of a bully boy. In the trade he was what we call a good 'on top' fighter. If he knew he was in charge he would show no mercy, but he could become surprisingly tame and unadventurous if he sensed he had met his match. A real Jekyll and Hyde character, and nobody was ever quite sure which face he was going to show in the ring.

I have to add here that later in our careers I got to like and understand Brian better, but there was no love lost between us in our early days when we were both ambitious not only to get to the top but to stay there. We'd both had good amateur careers. I had managed to win the ABA light-heavyweight championship two years on the trot, and London – then boxing under the name of Brian Harper – captured the Empire heavyweight title in Vancouver in 1954.

It was inevitable that we were going to meet as pros, and after a lot of hype we were matched in a non-title ten-rounder at the old Empress Hall on 1 May 1956. The fight was promoted by that lovely bloke Freddie Mills, but I don't think he did very good business with it because he paid out more than came in at the box office. The public, in the South at least, had not really warmed to London and I'd blotted my copybook six months earlier by dropping a points decision to Joe Erskine in a British title eliminator. It was the second defeat of my career. Italian Uber Bacilieri had stopped me in two rounds with a cut eye at Harringay on 26 April 1955. I got my revenge in seven rounds five months later, but the injury he'd caused to my old mince pie was to become a curse that would haunt me throughout my career.

The first fight with Brian London was my 15th since

making my professional debut on 14 September 1954. He had won all 12 of his fights and was the betting favourite. Mind you, the superstitious among the fight fraternity (and you can include me in that category) thought Brian was pushing his luck by weighing in for his 13th fight at 13 st. 13 lb.! And it certainly was his unlucky night. It was a May Day fight and London was quickly giving out May Day distress signals.

Early in the first round I caught him with the best right-hand body shot I ever threw, and it dug in so deep that London gasped and dropped his guard. He was a wide open target and I followed up with my favourite left hook. It landed flush on his jaw and knocked him backwards into a neutral corner where only the ropes stopped him from going down. I ripped in another couple of left hooks and a right cross before referee Tommy Little pulled me off and steered a semi-conscious London back to his corner.

That night I was on top of the world but over the next 12 months I had the worst run of my career, while London – much to his credit – picked himself up and went from strength to strength.

I was like a climber falling down a mountain when just a fingertip from the summit. Peter Bates stopped me with a cut eye on 7 September 1956, after I had given him a real pasting. Then I was beaten in three successive championship contests. Joe Bygraves, a former victim of mine, caught me with a vicious body shot that knocked the wind out of me and I was counted out for the first time in my career in the ninth round of a British Empire title fight on 9 February 1957.

Three months later I became one of the many boxers who underestimated Sweden's Ingemar Johansson. He landed his bombshell of a right hand on my jaw in the fifth round of a European title fight in Stockholm and I took the ten-second count on my knees.

Then, to complete my heartbreak hat-trick, I was narrowly outpointed by Joe Erskine in a British and Empire champion-ship contest at Harringay on 17 September 1957. I waved

good riddance to 1957 with a two-fingered Harvey Smith salute.

I got back on the winning trail when I stopped giant Welshman Dick Richardson, who carelessly walked on to my left hook after cutting and dropping me in the eventful fifth round of an explosive fight at Porthcawl. Five weeks later, on 14 October 1958, I had one of the best victories of my career when I outpointed world-ranked American Zora Folley over ten rounds at Wembley Arena. This set up a return with dual champion Brian London, who just 14 days earlier had scored an equally impressive win over future world light-heavyweight champion Willie Pastrano.

The Fight

Despite my one-round win over London in 1956, I went into the British and Empire championship fight as the underdog. *Boxing News*, the trade paper, predicted a London victory in eight rounds and few pressmen were on my side. But it didn't bother me one iota. It's easy to punch out predictions on a typewriter, but the only thing that matters is the punches thrown in the ring. I was quite happy to be the second favourite because it meant I didn't have the extra pressure of being expected to win, and deep down – as I've said – I had the feeling that I was London's boss.

There was no early night for me in the return. In fact I had to call on all my reserves of strength, stamina and willpower to survive what I regard as, in retrospect, one of the toughest fights of my career. It wasn't so much London who made it hard for me as a nose injury that restricted my breathing from the second round.

I had blood pumping down from the top of my nostril and I kept swallowing it, and this meant I was coughing up my own blood for much of the fight. Sorry for this technicolor stuff but boxing ain't a sport for the fainthearted. It's a hard game that separates the men from the boys and I believe both London and I proved ourselves men of some substance that night.

I relied almost exclusively on my left jab, sticking it through London's unsound defence literally hundreds of times during 15 exhausting rounds. He kept bulldozing forward but could never get me in range for long enough to land more than a couple of blows with each attack.

London, who at 14 st. 13 lb. was exactly a stone heavier than when we had first fought in 1956, opened two cuts under my right eye but, thank gawd, my dodgy scar tissue above the eye didn't reopen so my vision was never impaired. In return I opened a jagged cut over London's right eye and sometimes landed as many as 20 punches, mostly straight lefts, without reply. I must have given Brian a right old going over because he was so bemused at the end of the 14th round that he raised my hand thinking the fight was over.

He had merely given spectators a preview of the result because Welsh referee Ike Powell officially raised my hand at the end of the 15th. I had won by a mile and had made my dream of becoming British champion a reality. It was a title I was to keep proudly in my care for the next 12 years until it was nicked off me by Joe Bugner. But that's another story.

The Aftermath

London took his punishment like a man and I liked him a lot better after the brawl was over. In fact we became such good pals that we used to send each other good luck telegrams before major fights. We met once more, this time on his manor in Manchester on 24 February 1964. It was very much a repeat of our 1959 contest, with me keeping London on the end of my left even though I banged it up and bruised it early in the fight. I was a runaway points winner after a 15-

round contest in which the vacant European championship was at stake as well as my British and Empire titles.

I made my own little bit of history that night by becoming the first heavyweight for more than 50 years to win two Lonsdale Belts outright, and London sportingly told the Press: 'Henry's won me outright as well and can take me home and hang me over his mantlepiece.'

London remains the only British heavyweight to have made two challenges for the world title against different champions. He defied a ban by the British Boxing Board of Control, and went to Indianapolis for a tilt at the title then held by Floyd Patterson. On 1 May 1959 he was knocked out in the 11th round after a negative display during which he managed to land barely a dozen worthwhile blows. His challenge against Muhammad Ali at Earls Court seven years later lasted just two and a half rounds before he folded under a combination of punches from a champion who had hardly broken sweat.

In both his world championship contests London showed the unacceptable face of pugilism, the one the public disliked and distrusted. Yet there were many fights in which he showed the face of a brave and talented boxer who, on his night, was probably as good as any heavyweight Britain has ever produced. But too many times his nights turned into nightmares.

For the Record

Henry Cooper

Born Westminster, 3 May 1934.
Ht.: 6 ft. 2 in. Wt.: 13 st. 7½ lb.
ABA light-heavyweight champion 1952, 1953.
Turned professional 1954. Manager: Jim Wicks.
Honours: British, European and Commonwealth champion.
    Winner of three Lonsdale Belts outright.
Record: 55 fights, 40 wins, 1 draw, 14 losses (4KOs); 29 inside-the-distance wins (7 KOs).

Brian London

Born Blackpool 19 June 1934.
Ht.: 6 ft. Wt.: 14 st. 13 lb.
ABA and Empire Games heavyweight champion, 1954.
Turned professional 1955. Manager: his father, Jack London, and later L. Phillips.
Honours: British and Commonwealth heavyweight champion.
Record: 58 fights, 37 wins, 1 draw, 20 losses (3 KOs); 25 inside-the-distance wins (13 KOs).

Co-incidence note: both Brian London and I had our last fights against Joe Bugner. London retired at the end of five rounds against Bugner on 12 May 1970. I hung up my gloves after I was adjudged to have been outpointed by Bugner on 16 March 1971 (see chapter 15).

5

The Fight: Ingemar Johansson v. Floyd
Patterson
The Date: 26 June 1959
The Venue: Yankee Stadium, New York

The Build-up

I could have told Floyd Patterson he was walking into a
minefield when he agreed to defend his world heavyweight
crown against Sweden's Ingemar Johansson. Along with a
procession of European heavyweights I had felt the full weight
of the mighty right hand that became known as 'Ingo's
Bingo'.

Johansson knocked me out in the fifth round of a European
championship defence on an open-air promotion in Stockholm
on 19 May 1957. I can't describe the path the punch took,
simply because I didn't see it. I was backed in a corner and
had a blinding sun shining in my eyes. All I know is how it
felt. It was as if somebody had whacked me across the jaw
with a baseball bat. Bingo!

Patterson and his cautious manager Cus D'Amato, like so
many of us, completely miscalculated Johansson's ability.
The Swede just didn't look a class fighter. His left jab was a
pawing punch which from outside the ring seemed novice-

like, but when you were in there facing him it quickly became apparent that this was just a range-finder for his 'say good-night' right. Opponents used to think they could brush the left jab aside, which is exactly what he wanted them to think. As they forced their way forward he would be waiting to ambush them with a right hand that was used exclusively as a counter-punch. So it is easy to see how the Patterson camp managed to underestimate him. He looked so ordinary in the ring, and his life-style outside it lured people into thinking he was less than fully committed to the tough business of boxing.

Ingemar proved – at least for a couple of years – that he could burn the candle at both ends and still turn people's lights out with his 'Hammer of Thor' punching power. He was a good-looking guy with a big dimple in his chin and a winning smile. Nothing was going to stop him enjoying the good life and he led a playboy existence even when in training for major fights. It was the norm for him to go nightclubbing and dancing into the early hours during the build-up for championship contests and his beautiful 'secretary' Birgit – later his wife – used to accompany him on big fight trips and stay with him at his training camps.

Each to his own, but this sort of preparation would have been like poison to me. I liked to give total concentration to my training and I know Floyd Patterson had the same sort of approach to a fight. Seeing how Johansson behaved outside the ring helped strengthen his belief that he was facing an easy defence of his championship. Mind you, I think Ingemar deliberately exaggerated his playboy image while in the United States to try to kid Patterson that he was more interested in fun than fighting.

There had been little fun in Patterson's life. Born in Waco, North Carolina, on 4 January 1935, Floyd had come up the hard way. He was the third of 11 children and after moving to the tough area of Brooklyn he got into bad company and was sent to a rehabilitation school for juvenile delinquents. As for so many kids who have wandered on to the wrong side of the tracks, boxing proved the salvation for Patterson. When he was 14 he followed two older brothers to a New York gymnasium run by Cus D'Amato. He became hooked on the sport and D'Amato encouraged him to take it up seriously.

I was the light-heavyweight member of the British team in the 1952 Olympics in Helsinki, and after dropping a split points decision to a Russian I was able to take a close look at some of the other competitors. Patterson was the middle-weight representative for the United States and looked a million dollars on his way to the gold medal. Sweden's heavy-weight was an unimpressive, pedestrian-looking boxer called Ingemar Johansson. He reached the final only to suffer the humiliation of being disqualified against American Ed Sanders for allegedly 'not giving of his best'. (Many years later the Olympic Committee quite rightly wiped that slur out of the record books and presented him with the silver medal that had been withheld after he had been thrown out of the ring in disgrace.)

Both Patterson and Johansson turned professional after the Olympics. The Swedebasher became European heavyweight champion on 30 September 1956, when – in his 15th pro fight – he knocked out Italian holder Franco Cavicchi in 13 rounds in Milan. Two months later, on 30 November 1956, Patterson became the youngest heavyweight champion of all time when, aged 21 years 11 months, he knocked out Archie Moore in five rounds in a fight for the title vacated by Rocky Marciano.

It was Patterson's 32nd contest and he had won them all apart from a points defeat by ring-wise former world light-heavyweight champion Joey Maxim in a 'learning' contest.

Patterson had exceptionally fast fists and launched sudden, two-handed attacks from behind a high guard that became known as his 'peek-a-boo' style. He did not have the best of physiques for what was to become the era of the super-heavyweights. He stood barely six feet tall, weighed under 13½ stone and had a short reach of 71 inches. There were times when he would lunge forward with both feet off the ground in an effort to get maximum power into his punches, but it was a dangerous method of attack that left him open to counter blows, and in seven of his title bouts he was knocked down 16 times.

Cus D'Amato, making lots of enemies in the political jungle that is world heavyweight boxing in the United States, managed Patterson with a caution bordering on the paranoid. He cold-shouldered the legitimate contenders and steered Floyd through successful defences against Tommy Jackson, Pete Rademacher (the 1956 Olymic champion making his professional debut), Roy Harris and Britain's Brian London before agreeing to take on Ingemar Johansson. The European champion had just recorded his 21st successive victory by knocking out world-ranked American contender Eddie Machen in one round in Gothenburg. The Patterson camp thought he had just got lucky with a wild right-hand punch!

The Fight

Johansson duped the American Press as well as Patterson. They wrote him off as a no-hoper after watching him in lethargic training sessions when the crafty Swede kept his right hand under wraps. He talked about his right as if it was something separate from the rest of his body. 'It is a gift from the Gods,' he said. 'It is mystic and moves faster than the eye can see. I do not tell it when to go. Suddenly, boom! It lands like toonder.' Hard-bitten Yankee sportswriters thought they were being given ticket-selling spiel and, when the fight was postponed for twenty-four hours because of a thunderstorm, they thought that was the only 'toonder' they were going to experience.

Patterson was giving a stone in weight to the half-inch taller Swede, but the betting boys thought nothing of this and made him a firm 5–1 favourite to retain his title. I myself fancied the champion to win because I thought he would punch too quickly for a sometimes plodding opponent, but I had a gut feeling that he might be treating Johansson too lightly. How will he react, I wondered, if and when Ingo's Bingo lands on his jaw?

The first round was nearly over before Johansson unleashed his right for the first time. It clipped Patterson's left ear and caused him no undue consternation. The champion edged the first two undistinguished rounds, and there had been no sign of the 'toonder' storm heading his way.

Patterson sent two lefts to the head early in the third round and was standing square on as Johansson pawed with that range-finding left and then launched his right on an arc over the champion's lowered left. It exploded on Patterson's jaw and he went down as if shot. For a moment it looked all over as referee Ruby Goldstein started the count, but the champion pulled himself up into a sitting position and then on to his knees before rising at nine on suddenly elasticated legs. The next minute and a half provided some of the most sensational and in a way farcical action ever witnessed in a world heavy-weight championship contest.

Patterson didn't know whether he was in New York or Timbuktu and started on a wobbly course back towards his corner as if he thought the round had finished. Johansson, anxious to finish it there and then, threw a left and a following right that landed on the back of Patterson's neck. They were strictly speaking illegal blows but the champion had only himself to blame for turning his back, not that he knew which way he was facing.

Patterson went back down on his knees, held on to the middle rope and stared vacantly out at the roaring crowd as if he was the spectator and they the main attraction. Somehow he climbed up again at nine but was quickly knocked back down by a challenger who was bowling his punches in like Freddie Trueman on the rampage. Patterson was up and down like a yo-yo and took seven counts before Ruby

Goldstein at last came to his rescue after having given him more than enough chance to recover his shattered senses.

The world had a new heavyweight champion. Johansson was the first Swede ever to win the title and the first European holder of the championship since Primo Carnera 25 years earlier. 'It was just a matter of time before I landed with my toonder right,' said the new champion. American's press corps were nearly as thunderstruck as Patterson.

The Aftermath

Patterson and Johansson tied up the world championship between them for the next two years, which all other contenders, me included, thought was a disgraceful monopoly. They met in a return at the Polo Grounds, New York, on 20 June 1960, and this time a grimly determined Patterson created history by becoming the first world heavyweight champion to regain the title. He knocked Johansson's spark out with a cracking left hook to the jaw in the fifth round after the Swede had been floored for a nine count.

The 'decider' was staged in Miami on 13 March 1961. Patterson settled it once and for all by knocking out Johansson in the sixth round after taking two counts early in a hectic contest. Patterson had proved he had great character to go with his talent, but his 'bogey man' was waiting around the corner for him in the menacing shape of Sonny Liston (see chapter 7).

Johansson returned to Sweden some £1½ million richer from the three battles with Patterson, but he was still hungry for another crack at the world championship. He got back on the title trail by beating first Joe Bygraves and then detonating the old Ingo Bingo on Dick Richardson's jaw to regain the European championship he had given up after winning the world crown.

Johansson's chief backer, publisher and promoter Eddie

Alhqvist, was ready to set up a title fight with Sonny Liston once Ingemar had chalked up what they thought would be a routine victory over my old rival Brian London in Stockholm on 21 April 1963.

But it didn't work as planned. Johansson won on points over 12 rounds but he was the last person to know of his victory. London landed a volley of thumping blows in the dying moments of the fight and Ingemar was flat on his back when the bell saved him from a knock-out defeat.

It was too close for Johansson's comfort and he wisely decided to call it a day at the age of 31 and after a 28-fight career during which he caused some earthquaking shocks with his 'toonder' and lightning right. Ingo's Bingo pulled many a full house.

Both Johansson and Patterson were always a credit to boxing with their pleasant personalities away from the ring, and they maintained popularity long after throwing their parting shots. They both competed in the New York marathon in 1982 and completed the course, Patterson finishing a short distance ahead – which was the way it was in their three-fight world title marathon that spanned three years and made them both a fortune.

For the Record

Ingemar Johansson

Born Gothenburg, 22 September 1932.
Ht.: 6 ft. ½ in. Wt.: 14 st.
Turned professional 1952 after being disqualified in the 1952
    Olympic heavyweight final (finally received his silver medal
    in 1982). Advised by Eddie Alhqvist.
Honours: World and European heavyweight champion.
Record: 28 fights, 26 wins, 2 losses (2 KOs); 18 inside-the-distance
    wins (11 KOs).

Floyd Patterson

Born Waco, North Carolina, 4 January 1935.
Ht.: 6 ft. Wt.: 13 st. 2 lb.
1952 Olympic middleweight champion.
Turned professional 1952. Managed by Cus D'Amato.
Honours: the youngest ever world heavyweight champion at 21 years 11 months. First man to regain the heavyweight crown.
Records: 64 fights, 55 wins, 1 draw, 8 losses (2 KOs); 40 inside-the-distance wins (16 KOs).

6
The Fight: Henry Cooper v. Joe Erskine
The Date: 17 November 1959
The Venue: Earls Court

The Build-up

If Joe Erskine had been able to punch his weight I reckon he would have been heavyweight champion of the world. Strictly from my point of view I'm relieved that he couldn't whack all that hard because we fought each other eight times and he presented me with enough problems as it was.

They breed 'em tough down at the Tiger Bay end of Cardiff and Joe was a tough Taff, all right. He was built like a Welsh backrow forward yet was as light on his feet as a ballet dancer.

They could have created the description 'poker face' for old Joe, for whom I harbour a lot of affection despite our long-running rivalry in the ring. We used to be billeted together in our early days in the army when we were doing our National Service and our favourite past-time was playing cards. Joe could be holding a full house or a ten high and you would never guess it. He was as expressionless as the Sphinx. And that was just what he was like in the ring. I hit him with some of the hardest punches I ever threw but you would never know it from the look on his face. He was a cunning fox of a boxer who never showed emotions, and he had more natural boxing skill than any British heavyweight I have seen before or since.

Our careers ran parallel like two express trains and every now and then we found ourselves on the same track. Our lines crossed for the first time in the semi-finals of the ABA light-heavyweight championship in 1952. It was a battle of the left jabs and I just managed to get the better of him over three evenly balanced rounds which neutrals said presented traditional British boxing at its best.

We were both upright boxers who liked to move about behind a stiff left jab and keep the action at long range. Where I always had an advantage over Joe was that I could hook off the jab which meant I carried the heavier ammunition, but I'd have to own up to him being the cleverer boxer. He had such good rhythm and neat footwork that he could nullify the big punchers by keeping them off balance and out of distance; and he was a master at swaying and rolling on the ropes, letting opponents punch themselves out by hitting thin air. Mind you, it was a dangerous practice that brought him a lot of trouble later in his career when the lead started getting into his legs.

Our styles didn't change very much from when we first fought, although I think I developed my punching power and stepped up my workrate to the body whereas Joe stuck to his stylish jab-and-move tactics. We met twice more as amateurs, both of them army tournament contests, and we won one each on points. So when we both turned professional in 1954 the score stood at two—one in my favour.

Our first fight with a purse rather than a pot at stake came at Harringay on 15 November 1955, in an official eliminator for the British championship. It was a repeat of our amateur contests, only this time spread over ten rounds, and it was Joe whose hand was raised by the referee at the end. I concentrated too much on conserving my energy in the early part of the fight and was unable to make up lost ground. I had Joe in trouble a couple of times with left hooks but the wily bugger rolled, weaved and danced his way out of bother. I banged my left hand up on his tough old Welsh bonce in the seventh round, but no excuses. Joe deserved his win.

That wasn't my night and as a superstitious sort I couldn't help reflecting on the fact that it was my thirteenth fight. On the way home our car, a black, second-hand Ford Prefect and our pride and joy, got smashed into at a crossroads and we somersaulted twice. My twin brother George was driving and in the back were our elder brother Bernie and his wife Cory, who was six months pregnant. All four (or five) of us scrambled out shaken but unhurt. The bloke in the car that hit us thought I was badly injured because of the cuts and bruises on my face. But this had been the work of Joe Erskine's fists and was nothing to do with the crash. Looking back on it, I suppose I have to call it our lucky night because we could so easily have been written off along with the car.

My fifth fight with Joe came in my black year of 1957. I had been knocked out by a body blow from Joe Bygraves in a British Empire title fight on 19 February and then took the full count after Ingo's Bingo had landed on my jaw in a European championship contest against Ingemar Johansson in Stockholm on 19 May. Joe had beaten fellow-Welshman Johnny Williams for the British title vacated by Don Cockell and put it on the line against me in London on 17 September.

My confidence wasn't exactly sky-high and again I made too cautious a start, allowing Joe to build an early lead. But I came back strongly and there were several times when even Joe's poker face couldn't hide the fact that I had hurt him. I was choked when the referee held up Joe's hand at the end of the 15th round because I thought I'd done just enough to have nicked the verdict.

Both Joe and I had managers who could claim the fastest tongue in the West. My guiding light was a witty, street-wise Cockney called Jim Wicks but known to everybody in the

fight game as 'The Bishop' because of his benign looks. His mind was scalpel sharp and he could have sold postcards to the Arabs. I looked on him like a favourite uncle and was happy to leave all my boxing affairs in his capable hands. Joe was managed by a colourful Jewish Welshman called Benny Jacobs, a master at banging the publicity drum and of filling reporter's notebooks with outrageous, ticket-selling statements.

Because we left Jim and Benny to do much of the talking for us, the public got the impression that there was bitterness and enmity between Joe and me. But that was all hocus pocus created by our managers. Outside the ring Joe and I were good pals and inside the ropes we had total respect for each other.

Of our eight fights, the one I remember above all others is the sixth, when I at last proved that I was the undisputed guv'nor.

The Fight

I was in the champion's corner when Joe and I met for the sixth time, at Earls Court on 17 November 1959. Joe had lost his championship to Brian London and I in turn had relieved London of both the British and Empire titles.

There was no denying that Erskine deserved the chance to try to regain the British crown but he had never met me in more determined or confident mood. He weighed in at 13 st. 10 lb., which gave him a four-pounds weight advantage, but I was always happiest when boxing at 13 st. 6 or 7 lb. and I felt superbly fit and raring to go.

I had made up my mind to try to hurt him early, rather than hang around as in our previous professional battles. I was handicapped by a cut in the first round but had the satisfaction of knowing I had really stunned him with a couple of good left hooks. In fact I had Joe grabbing hold of me while he cleared his head. He couldn't kid me with his poker face this time.

There was a controversial finish to the end of the fifth round. Right through my career I specialized in throwing a hook off a left jab, that is leading with the left and then all in the same movement throwing the same hand but this time from an angle. I had pierced Joe's guard with the jab and was into the reflex action of throwing the hook when the bell rang. Joe relaxed and my punch continued on its way and landed flush on his jaw.

Anybody who ever saw me box would know that I never once committed a deliberate foul in the ring. This was a complete accident but Benny Jacobs made a meal of it. He came diving into the ring and demanded that Scottish referee Eugene Henderson should disqualify me. Mr Henderson was closer to the incident than anybody else apart from Joe and I, and he knew that the punch had started before the bell. He quite rightly ordered Benny back to his corner but Benny had made such a fuss that it planted the thought in some minds that I had gained an unfair advantage.

It was the first time in all my fights with Erskine when I felt in complete control despite the aggravation of the cut over my right eye. Joe was also cut, over his left eye, and as the fight moved into the last third I knew I'd got him going.

The end came in the 12th round and it was one of the most frightening experiences I have ever known in the ring. Joe was doing one of his rolling and weaving acts on the ropes but he was tired and lacked his usual split-second timing. I caught him with a cracker of a left hook to the jaw and he slid down the ropes for the first count either of us had ever taken in our six meetings. He was up at seven and I quickly moved in with a two-fisted attack that sent him down for another seven count.

I wish the referee had moved in because Joe was in no position to defend himself but I was waved forward and this time I let fly with a left-right combination followed by a left hook that carried every ounce of my strength. Poor Joe fell backwards, the top-half of his body crashing under the middle rope. He was arched backwards over the bottom rope like a giant violin bow, and he was out to the world. The referee wisely didn't bother to count but stopped the fight there and then, and waved for assistance to get Joe disentangled from the ropes.

Even in this sweet moment of victory I felt sick because I thought Joe had broken his back. Jim Wicks felt the same way and was shivering with fright when I returned to the corner. Thank God Joe recovered after some treatment from the ringside doctor and suffered only bruising to his back.

Like I say, for all our rivalry Joe and I were good buddies and the last thing I wanted was to see him seriously injured. Boxing is a hard, hard sport, but you'd be suprised how close and caring opponents become.

The Aftermath

Crafty old Benny Jacobs made the most of the punch that I landed after the bell in the fifth round and kicked up such a stink that we had to give Joe another crack at the titles. We fought at Wembley on 21 March 1961, and it lasted only fifteen minutes. My left hand was never out of his face and both of his eyes were cut and closing when his corner took the referee's advice and retired him at the end of the fifth round. It was a memorable moment for me because this third successful championship defence won me my first Lonsdale Belt outright.

Just over a year later Joe and I were at it again, this time in Manchester and again my British and Empire titles were at stake. He was past his best and very puffy around the eyes and he lacked the mobility that had made him such a difficult target in his prime. I concentrated on shovelling as many lefts as I could through his defence as in the previous fight and I closed one of his eyes and gashed the other before the referee stopped the one-sided traffic in the ninth round.

It was our eighth and last fight, so I finished 5–3 ahead in our series that spanned the best ten years of our fighting lives. But neither of us were ever really a loser because we won each other's friendship and respect.

Joe battled on for a couple of years after our final fight but was never the same major force in the game, and he retired in 1964 after a points defeat by Billy Walker, a fighter who would have struggled to lay a glove on him when he was at his majestic peak.

I'm sorry to say Joe has been in poor health in recent years. If he reads this I hope he will remember with warmth our many rounds together, which were always fought in a sporting spirit – despite what Benny Jacobs claimed about the punch that landed after the bell! Good on you, Joe. You were a gem of a boxer and a real man's man. If you'd had something like my hammer in your hand you would, my old son, have been champion of the world.

For the Record

Joe Erskine

Born Cardiff, 26 January 1934.
Ht.: 6 ft. Wt.: 13 st. 10 lb.
ABA heavyweight champion 1953.
Turned professional 1954. Managed by Benny Jacobs.
Honours: British and Empire heavyweight champion.
Record: 54 fights, 45 wins, 1 draw, 8 losses (1 KO); 15 inside-the-distance wins (2 KOs).

7

The Fight: Sonny Liston v. Floyd Patterson
The Date: 25 September 1962
The Venue: Comiskey Park, Chicago

The Build-up

Sonny Liston was the meanest, the moodiest and also the most misunderstood world heavyweight champion of all time. And in the end he finished up as the saddest of all the champions. He was painted as an out-and-out villain, a hoodlum heavyweight who ran with gangsters and showed a flagrant disregard for the law.

There is no doubt that he did keep dubious company and many of his formative years were spent on the wrong side of the law, but I believe he deserves a charitable assessment of his career and his conduct, which need to be judged in the context of his early upbringing.

We're all of us shaped by the environment in which we grow up and Liston started right at the bottom of the heap. He was one of 25 children fathered during two marriages by Tobe Liston, a poverty-stricken Arkansas cotton farmer for whom Sonny had only contempt. His real name was Charles but apparently his father called all his sons Sonny because there were so many kids around that he couldn't remember their names. How about that for creating an identity crisis?

At the age of about 13 Sonny ran away to St Louis and lived by his wits in the city streets, where he often stole so that he could buy food and clothes. I say he was 'about 13' because he was never sure of his date of birth. The record books give it as 8 May 1934, but it was more likely two years earlier. He had no schooling to speak of and he was unable to read or write.

His reputation for being sullen and uncommunicative in later years was caused by an in-built suspicion and distrust because he'd had so many kicks in life. Liston had been sent to the equivalent of one of our borstals after getting caught breaking and entering just a year after arriving in St Louis. Then in 1950 he was sentenced to a five-year term in the Missouri State Penitentiary for robbery. After two years he was transferred to a farm prison and then, in October 1952, he was paroled on the understanding that he concentrated on boxing, a sport for which he had shown an enthusiasm and natural ability while in the prison gymnasium.

Once again boxing had given a lost soul a platform upon which he could find an identity and self-respect. Within a year Sonny had won a Golden Gloves title, and he switched to the professional ring in 1953.

He won 14 of his first 15 fights, seven of his victories coming by the knock-out route. His one set-back was an eight-round points defeat by Marty Marshall who broke his jaw in the second round. In two rematches Liston knocked Marshall out in six rounds and then outpointed him on 6 March 1956.

His career was just taking off in a big way when he got involved in an argument with a policeman over a parking ticket. The policeman finished up in hospital with a broken leg and seven stitches in a cut over his eye. Liston finished up in prison for nine months. When he came out of jail he found his opponents were not only in the ring. He was stopped and questioned by police more than a hundred times and was arrested 19 times on charges that never led to anything but aggravation. Sonny Liston was not the most popular person in St Louis as far as the police were concerned. In fact he really got the St Louis blues, and it helped breed his brooding personality. He moved to Philadelphia in a bid to make a new life for himself but many of the dodgy acquaintances that he'd latched on to during his law-busting days continued to cling to him.

He made his comeback after 20 months out of the ring on 29 January 1958, and stopped Billy Hunter in two rounds. By the end of the year he had disposed of another seven opponents and had taken his record to 22 wins in 23 fights. He had four fights in 1959, stopping four world title contenders – Mike DeJohn (four rounds), Cleveland Williams (three rounds), Nino Valdes (three rounds) and Willi Besmanoff (six rounds).

Standing 6 ft. 1 in. and weighing around 15 st. 4 lb., Liston was an awesome sight when letting fly with his big bombs. He had a phenomenal reach of 84 inches and a fist measurement of 15 inches – larger than any champion in heavyweight history. My manager Jim Wicks got to hear about him early in his career from one of his many contacts in the United States and was told not to have anything to do with him because 'he could break opponents in half with one punch'. When anybody ever mentioned the possibility of Liston as an opponent for me, Jim used to say: 'We [he always used the royal "we"] don't want to meet this geezer Liston walking down the street let alone in the ring.'

After five more victories in 1960 Liston was an obvious contender for the world championship but the boxing establishment was terrified of his out-of-the-ring reputation. Boxing has not got the greatest image but the powers-that-be like to be seen to be trying to run everything in an above-suspicion manner. There was an official inquiry as well as many media investigations into Liston's gangster connections and he was forced to change his managerial team, although he never shook off the allegations that he was still being manipulated by undesirable associates.

Cus D'Amato, Floyd Patterson's manager, wanted no part of a defence against Liston who had taken his winning streak to 33 out of 34 fights. In fact he was looking across the Atlantic at a certain bloke called Henry Cooper as a more acceptable opponent. Who was I to argue? But Patterson's pride forced him to overrule D'Amato. Floyd was desperately anxious to be accepted as a great champion and he knew that he would never get the public recognition he hungered for if he ducked the obvious No. 1 contender. Furthermore Liston helped to push Patterson into accepting the fight by taunting him with accusations that he was frightened of him. The champion took the bait and agreed to give 'big, bad' Sonny his chance.

The Fight

The championship contest was originally scheduled for New York but a promoting licence was refused because of the controversy over Liston's gangster links. The fight was switched to Chicago and the challenger said with chilling confidence: 'Don't matter where it is. My punches are just as hard in Chicago as in New York.' Liston was not particularly articulate but he had a store of good one-liners. When asked which referee he would prefer he said: 'It don't matter as long as he can count up to ten.'

All the pre-fight hype projected it as a battle between 'Saint' Patterson and 'Sinner' Liston. 'In the films the good guy always wins, but this ain't no film and this is one bad guy who ain't gonna lose,' said Sonny. The crowd went along with the Good Guy v. Bad Guy theme and booed 'Old Stone Face' Liston into the ring as loudly as they cheered Patterson.

The champion looked like a middleweight compared with

the magnificently sculptured challenger who at 15 st. 3 lb. had a weight advantage of nearly two stone.

In the opening moments there was no hint of the sensation to come. Liston missed with a jab and Patterson missed with a hook. It was quickly obvious that Sonny's massive reach was going to present the champion with problems. He tried one of his peculiar leaping-in rights but was way out of distance. Liston was snapping his left out at surprising speed and the punches were thudding through Floyd's peek-a-boo guard as if he had no defence.

Patterson tried crouching to make himself less of a target but still the lefts – jabs and hooks – came pounding through. He then moved to close quarters and fired a tattoo to the body but he was forced to give ground as Liston landed the first really heavy blow, a right to the kidney region.

The huge challenger was pushing Patterson around as if he were a little boy who had wandered into the ring by mistake. A sudden right uppercut lifted the champion off his feet and he fell into a clinch. The fight was only just over a minute old but already Patterson looked totally overwhelmed and outgunned.

Liston didn't seem to be putting any big effort into his punches but every one that landed had Floyd looking distressed. Two beautifully timed left hooks sent Patterson sideways and he instinctively grabbed the top strand of the rope. Liston followed up with two rib-bending rights and then a clubbing right-left combination to the head.

Patterson collapsed slowly to the canvas like a puppet that has had its strings cut away. As he started his descent a long left hook partially lifted him before he fell almost in slow-motion on to his side.

The champion – now within the last ten seconds of his reign – rolled over and crawled to the centre of the ring as referee Frank Sikora shouted the count into his dazed face. Patterson was on his feet as the count reached ten but was in no position to defend himself and he groped the referee's arm as Sikora signalled a knock-out.

It was all over in two minutes six seconds. Sonny Liston had moved from the bottom of the heap to the very top. It was the first time that a champion had won the title with a first-round knockout. Only Tommy Burns (1 min. 28 secs. v. Jem Roche) and Joe Louis (2 mins. 4 secs. v Max Schmeling) had scored quicker wins in world heavyweight title fights. 'Next time I'll do it just as quick,' said the ex-convict turned champion as they prepared for the inevitable return.

A desperately disappointed and ashamed Patterson left the stadium by a back exit wearing a false moustache and glasses so that nobody would recognize him and perhaps ridicule him. The fact that he had bothered to pack this theatrical disguise says nothing for his confidence going into the fight. No wonder some people called this complex character Freud Patterson.

The Aftermath

Liston's prediction that he would win just as quickly in the return was wrong – by four seconds. They met in the gambling city of Las Vegas on 22 July 1963, and Liston became a ruthless two-armed bandit. He was completely contemptuous of Patterson and knocked him about the ring as if he was half his size and weight.

Clubbing lefts and rights had Patterson down on his knees inside the first minute. He wobbled up at four and stood tottering on rubber legs as referee Harry Krause completed the mandatory eight count. Poor Patterson was reliving a nightmare of pain and humiliation as Liston moved menacingly forward, brushed aside a brave right as if he was swatting a fly and then threw his own right to Floyd's unguarded head. The former champion sagged to the canvas again, this time managing to haul himself up at five but with the glazed, lost look on his face of a man going to the gallows.

Liston quickly completed the execution. Two right crosses to the head followed by a scything left sent the pulverized Patterson to the canvas for the third and last time where he took the full count with his head cradled on a twitching elbow.

The official time given was two minutes ten seconds and Liston was still the champ. 'Will you defend against Cassius Clay next?' the champion was asked.

'That young pup?' Liston replied with an icy stare. 'What d'you want . . . to get me arrested for murder?'

Patterson didn't don a disguise when leaving his dressing-room this time. He knew he had to learn to live with himself and he regained his self-respect with two brave shows against Muhammad Ali and one of his more impressive performances was against a bloke I know better than anybody. Me.

We fought at Wembley on 20 September 1966, and I obtained explosive, first-hand evidence that his were the fastest fists in the business. I'd been giving at least as good as Floyd had been dishing out in the first three rounds but was overwhelmed early in the fourth by a lightning combination of left and right hooks.

I went down for nine with blood streaming from my old hooter. Blimey, I thought, I'd better do something about this and so I went looking for him with my left hook. But he found me instead with a corker of a straight right and it was 'goodnight nurse'. I'd been hit harder in my life but never with quicker punches.

Floyd Patterson was a top-quality fighter, but never a great champion because he simply wasn't big enough and had a suspect chin. He will always be haunted by the memory of Sonny Liston who, you got the feeling, could have beaten Floyd a hundred times out of a hundred. But Floyd will always be remembered as 'the Good Guy'. He was (and is) a smashing bloke who has ironed out all his psychological problems and now, as a New York Commissioner, gives a lot back to the game he served with such distinction.

For the Record

Sonny Liston

Born St Francis County, Arkansas, 8 May 1932 (or 1934).
Ht.: 6 ft. 1 in. Wt.: 15 st. 4 lb.
Golden Gloves heavyweight champion 1953.
Turned professional 1953. Various managers.
Honours: world heavyweight champion 1962–4.
Record: 54 fights, 50 wins, 4 losses (2 KOs); 39 inside-the-distance
  wins (25 KOs).

8
The Fight: Cassius Clay v. Sonny Liston
The Date: 2 February 1964
The Venue: Miami Beach, Florida

The Build-up

An unfunny thing happened to Cassius Clay on his way to a world championship challenge against Sonny Liston. I whacked him on the whiskers with my favourite left hook and for a few dramatic moments it looked as if I had thrown a spanner – or, rather, a hammer – into the works.

The most talked-about punch that I ever threw came in the last seconds of the fourth round of a scheduled ten-rounder in the open air at Wembley Stadium on 18 June 1963. I've seen a few Cup Final goals scored there in my time but Wembley had never heard a roar quite like the one that greeted the sight of Clay falling backwards into the ropes.

I wonder how boxing history might have changed had I landed some ten seconds earlier? As it was, young Cassius was up and at my mercy at four, but just as I was about to try to deliver the *coup de grâce* the bell rang.

Some time-wasting chicanery by his wily cornerman Angelo Dundee helped give Clay precious extra seconds to recover.

One of his gloves had split and Dundee has since admitted making the tear in the glove worse so that they had to wait for a replacement. I'm not complaining, because it's exactly the sort of trick I would have expected my manager Jim Wicks to have got up to if it had been me who was in bother. All's fair in love, war and the fight game.

Anyway, Clay had completely recovered his senses by the time the fifth round finally got under way and he hit me with a stream of long lefts and rights that worsened a cut over my left eye and forced the referee to stop it. Clay, who was into his poetic predictions period, had said before the fight: 'After all the jive, Cooper will fall in five.' He'd got the round right, but I hadn't fallen. My spirit was still more than willing but my flesh was weak.

Little though he realized it at the time, I did Cassius a favour by knocking him down for the first time in his career. Among the ringside spectators was Liston's No. 1 adviser Jack Nilon, and seeing Clay floored convinced him that it was safe for Sonny to put his title on the line. It gave a world stage to possibly the greatest boxer and certainly the greatest sporting showman of the century: the one and only Cassius Marcellus Clay.

The descendant of a slave and the son of a signwriter, Clay was born in Louisville, Kentucky, on 17 January 1942. He had first revealed his outstanding ring skills as an 18-year-old amateur who won the US light-heavyweight title in 1960 and then collared the Olympic gold medal in Rome.

He became a chatterboxer when he turned professional immediately after the Games and was quickly dubbed the Louisville Lip as he drummed up business at the box-office with a tongue that was even quicker than his fists. A lot of people thought he was a big head as well as a big mouth, but his boasts were calculated to boost ticket sales and also to give himself a psychological advantage over opponents who fell for that sort of thing. I personally never worried about what my opponents had to say for themselves. The only thing

I was concerned about was what they did with the jab rather than the gab.

It was all a big act with Clay. Once the microphones were turned off, the notebooks put away and the cameras pointed in a different direction, he became quietly spoken and a really nice bloke to be with. I'll always have a warm spot for him and there's no doubt that he brought the world boxing scene alight and alive.

Clay quickly put together a sequence of eight successive victories at the start of his professional career and then introduced his great gimmick of nominating the round in which he would win his fights. He was as good a prophet as he was a fighter. Some of the fighters he faced were of the 'strictly an opponent' category, but Alonzo Johnson, Alex Miteff, Willie Besmanoff, Ageless Archie Moore and Doug Jones were no pushovers and they all fell in the nominated round apart from Jones, who was the only one who was still perpendicular at the end.

One target Clay missed was to take over from Floyd Patterson as the youngest heavyweight champion of all time. He was held up by the Liston–Patterson return match and he was just 39 days past his 22nd birthday when he got his chance of dethroning Liston.

Clay's victory over me was his 19th in succession and he then started a verbal campaign against Liston that many people thought bordered on the hysterical – and I don't mean funny. He invaded the champion's training quarters and teased him with taunts of 'Old Bear' and waved a bear trap in Liston's face. His poetic forecast was: 'I'm predicting as true as fate that the Big Bear will fall in eight.' He chased Liston all over town waving a banner inscribed: 'The Bear-Shooting Season is Open.' He got himself a megaphone and kept repeating over and over again for everybody to hear: 'I am the Greatest . . . I am the Greatest . . .'

It was great for box-office business but Liston was among those convinced that Clay was running scared. 'The kid's making a lot of noise to hide the fact that he's as scared as hell of me,' said the champion with the same sort of icy confidence he showed before the two fights with Patterson.

Clay ranted and raved so much at the weigh-in that there was a danger of the fight being called off because the Boxing Commission's chief physician diagnosed that he was emotionally unbalanced. Clever Gaseous Cassius had fooled everybody.

The Fight

From the first bell it was clear that Liston was not going to have it as easy as it had been against Patterson. For a start Clay was a moving target, and physically he was a match for the champion. Whereas Patterson had looked dwarfed, Clay at 6 ft. 3 in. had a two-inch height advantage, weighed just seven pounds less than the 15 st. 8 lb. Liston and could land from a distance with his 82-inch reach.

Liston, tipped by almost all the media experts to win in quick time, came forward throwing the same sort of punches that had pulverized Patterson. But this time they were hitting empty air as Clay back-pedalled behind a light but accurate left lead. Suddenly the challenger stopped his dancing, stood his ground and met the champion with a right lead, two powerful lefts and another right to the head. The sombre Liston blinked almost in disbelief as Clay jeered and sneered at him before getting back 'on his bike'. In the last minute of the round Clay landed six left jabs without reply. If the 'kid' was scared, he had a funny way of showing it.

Liston had experienced only two rounds of competitive boxing in the last two years and there were definite signs in those first three minutes of ring rust. He came out for the second round with a sense of purpose and determination that was missing in the first. He had obviously made up his mind that the time had come to squash his brash young opponent.

71

He thumped home a heavy left hook to the jaw but when he tried to follow up Clay backed away to the ropes and cleverly made him miss.

The champion continued to chase Clay and managed to pin him on the ropes and score heavily to the body and then to the head with two clubbing rights. But Clay was unhurt and soon back on his toes and moving back in a circle, making full use of the ring as Liston stalked him in menacing mood.

Clay was regularly on target with his jabs, and evidence that they were having effect came early in the third round when blood started to ooze from a gash below Liston's left eye, the first cut of his career.

The jabs continued to stream in from Clay in the fourth round and he seemed to be almost enjoying himself, grinning down at ringside spectators and taunting and teasing the champion with now-you-see-me-now-you-don't dancing tactics. Liston's left eye was beginning to swell and close and he appeared to be ageing by the minute.

Round five was sensational. Clay started to retreat with his hands down at his sides, not attempting to throw a punch and was plainly in distress. He was dabbing at his eyes with his gloves and looking apprehensively to trainer Angelo Dundee in his corner. But even though he was not throwing any leather himself he managed to avoid most of the punches hurled by the lumbering Liston as he positively skated backwards around the ring. It had to be one of the strangest rounds of boxing ever witnessed in a world heavyweight title fight.

It was later learned that Clay thought he was going blind because of a stinging pain in his eyes. Some embrocation used to staunch the cut under Liston's eye had got into the challenger's eyes. It led to a dramatic incident in the corner with Angelo Dundee having to drink from the bottle to prove to some of Clay's accusing black associates that it had not been tampered with. 'I thought your guys were going to kill me,' he later told Clay. 'They thought I had done something to the water.'

Clay recovered during the interval at the end of the fifth round and came out for the sixth full of his earlier zest and fire. He pumped jabs and hooks into the face of Liston, whose advance had now slowed considerably. The champion seemed to be conserving his energy ready for a long, hard night. There was little to choose between them when they returned to their corners at the end of the round. Liston's handlers huddled around him and suddenly it became apparent that something was wrong, although there had been no hint of trouble during the action. Clay was first to realize that Liston wasn't coming out for the seventh round and he was quickly off his stool and running round the ring with arms raised shouting: 'I am the Champ . . . I am the Greatest . . .'

The champion – or, rather, the ex-champion – had apparently dislocated his left shoulder as early as the first round and later said that his left hand had become so numb he couldn't feel it. Watching a re-run of the fight on video, I have noted that the last punch that Liston threw before his shock retirement was a big left hook. A funny thing to do if your shoulder is dislocated and your hand numb!

The Aftermath

It was such an unsatisfactory finish that it was rumoured that the Miami Beach Boxing Commission was going to hold up Liston's purse, but after a statement signed by eight doctors confirming that his shoulder was indeed damaged it was decided to pay him out.

Clay gave Liston the chance to regain the title at Lewiston, Maine, on 25 May 1965, and this time there was an even bigger and more confusing mystery surrounding the finish of the fight. Did I say fight? Farce would be a more fitting description.

It started and finished with the first punch thrown in anger. After nearly a minute of sparring, feinting and missing, back-pedalling by the champion and menacing looks from the challenger, Clay let go with a light left lead followed by a short right cross that landed high on Liston's left cheekbone. It looked a pretty good punch, but the sort that you see thrown and taken in dozens of fights without causing any undue distress. The effect on Liston was as if he had walked into thunderbolt of a punch. He collapsed to the canvas and rolled over on his back. Clay stood over him, shouting: 'Get up and fight you bum.'

Referee Jersey Joe Walcott, the former world champion who looked out of his depth when faced with this dramatic situation, failed to order Clay to a neutral corner and also failed to pick up the count correctly. The timekeeper tolled to ten before Liston almost reluctantly regained his feet and Clay came forward firing a salvo of wild punches. Meantime Nat Fleischer, the respected Editor of *Ring Magazine*, banged on the ring apron to attract Walcott's attention and told him that Liston had been down long enough to have been counted out twice.

Walcott turned and raced back in between the two fighters, pushed Liston back and raised Clay's arm in victory. He was still the champion in the last fight in which he was to answer to the name of Cassius Clay. In future he insisted on being known as Muhammad Ali.

The official time given for the fight was one minute exactly, a record for the heavyweight division. But a stop-watch on the video of the fight proves that it actually lasted 106 seconds, with Liston on the canvas for nearly half minute! I'm not sure poor old Sonny knew his own name that night. I've rarely seen a man looking so bemused, confused and sorry for himself.

He went on fighting for another five years, winning another 14 fights in succession. He rose to third place in the world rankings but blew his chances of another crack at the title when he was knocked out in the ninth round by Philadelphian Leotis Martin. Six months later, on 29 June 1970, he stopped highly rated Chuck Wepner in nine rounds to prove he was still a force to be reckoned with.

It was his last fight. He died, apparently from natural causes, in his Las Vegas apartment on New Year's Eve. Sadly, he lay dead at home for six days before his body was discovered by his wife. There were strong rumours that Sonny had been 'eliminated' by gangster associates but nobody was ever able to prove anything.

Sonny Liston, the saddest of all the world heavyweight champions, took his big fight secrets with him to his grave. Nobody will ever know exactly what went on in his mind and in the ring in his two controversial world title fights with Cassius Clay, alias Muhammad Ali.

For the Record

Cassius Clay (Muhammad Ali)

Born Louisville, Kentucky, 17 January 1942.
Ht.: 6 ft. 3 in. Wt.: 16 st.
US amateur and Olympic light-heavyweight champion, 1960.
Turned professional October 1960. Manager: Herbert Muhammad.
Honours: world heavyweight champion 1964–7, 1974–8, 1979. The only boxer to have won the heavyweight crown three times.
Record: 61 fights, 56 wins, 5 losses (no KOs); 37 inside-the-distance wins (29 KOs).

9

The Fight: Henry Cooper v. Johnny Prescott
The Date: 15 June 1965
The Venue: St Andrew's Football Stadium,
Birmingham

The Build-up

There was a queue of good-quality British heavyweights chasing my titles in the 1960s, Johnny Prescott being prominent among them. They called him Beau Brummie – the Beau Brummel of Birmingham – because of his good looks, sharp dress sense and his liking for the ladies. No end of stories used to circulate about Johnny and his playboy activities and once, when I saw him with the notorious Mandy Rice Davies wrapped round him at the ringside, I wondered how on earth he got his energy for fighting.

Mind you, I reckon he deserved any luck and good times that came his way after the lousy hand fate had dealt him in his early days. When he was just two, his father died on the Dunkirk beaches while serving with the Tank Corps, and his mother was killed in an air raid. So Johnny was sent to an orphanage until he was 13, when an uncle took him into his home.

He started taking boxing seriously while doing his National

Service in the army as a physical training instructor and he boxed for England as an amateur in 1961. He turned professional later that same year after being outpointed in the Midlands amateur championships by Swadlincote southpaw Jack Bodell, later to be his stablemate and another of my rivals.

In his first two years punching for pay Prescott racked up a score of victories including eight clean knock-outs. He had been beaten just once in 23 starts when he collided with the first of his Coopers – my twin brother George, who used to box under the name of Jim because there was already a George Cooper on the pro circuit.

George was a good banger who would have gone right to the top but for atrocious luck with injuries. They met in Birmingham on 22 March 1963, and George saw Prescott off in style, demolishing him in two rounds. Three months later Prescott had an even bigger disaster when his former sparring partner Alex Barrow, a big-punching Nigerian, stopped him in just 100 seconds.

Prescott got another hiding when he returned to the dressing-room, this time a severe tongue-lashing from his wise old manager George Biddles who told him: 'You're paying the price for being too much of a goodtime Charlie. If you want to get anywhere in this business you had better start becoming less of a ladykiller and more of a killer in the ring.'

The Biddles broadside had its desired effect and in his next fight Prescott avenged his defeat by Barrow with a convincing points victory. He followed this with two memorable battles against the highly touted new 'Golden Boy' of British boxing, Billy Walker. Prescott was stopped in the tenth and last round of their first thrilling fight, and then got off the canvas to win the return on points.

His performances against Walker won him a lot of favour with the fans and George Biddles, a veteran manager who had guided Hogan 'Kid' Bassey to the world featherweight title, started a tub-thumping verbal campaign to get Prescott a crack at my British and Empire titles.

Biddles kept pressing the point, perhaps with some justification, that the public were fed up with the Cooper-Erskine-London monopoly of the championships. I had made five successful defences of the British and Empire titles since taking them from Brian London in 1959. Three had been against Joe Erskine, another against London and I had knocked out Welshman Dick Richardson in five rounds of a title fight at Wembley in 1963. 'British boxing needs a new young heavyweight champion.' said Biddles. I was an 'old man' of 31 and itching for a first notch on a third Lonsdale Belt when Biddles got his wish and steered his man into a title fight with me. Prescott was two months off his 27th birthday.

The Fight

We were due to fight in the open air at Birmingham City's football ground at St Andrew's, but suffered the irritation of a two-day delay because of heavy rain. I was more anxious about the contest than I would usually have been because I was carrying the secret that negotiations had been all but completed for me to challenge Cassius Clay for the world heavyweight championship.

I knew I dare not let Prescott beat me because it could wreck the plans and the chance I had dreamt of since I was a kid pretending to be Joe Louis. I came in for the title defence at 13 st. 4 lb. which was just a couple of pounds lighter than I liked. Prescott was four pounds heavier, while I had a slight advantage in height and reach.

In the second half of my career I found I was not very clever at getting myself 'up' for certain fights. I dropped silly points decisions in pretty meaningless contests against Americans Roger Rischer and Amos Johnson, two opponents

78

I should have seen off in style. But I never had any problem getting myself into the right tough frame of mind for title fights, and the prospect of the return match with Clay – with the world championship on the line – made me doubly determined to see off Prescott's challenge.

Johnny had been specially coached for the fight by Jack Hood, a former European welterweight champion whose ring skills were legendary. He had learnt his lessons well and managed to stop me landing any really telling blows in the first half-dozen rounds, but I felt well in command and was patiently biding my time. He was dangerous with his head and opened a cut on my left cheekbone but it looked worse than it was. For the last half minute of each round Prescott was dropping his hands to his hips – Clay style – and dancing around the perimeter of the ring. I was sure the old master Jack Hood had not advised these tactics and I decided to make them work in my favour.

From the seventh round I started to concentrate on firing heavy shots to the body as Prescott dropped his hands. I was waiting for him to lead and then countered with hooks to the ribs that had him gasping and grunting with pain.

Early in the eighth round I threw a short left hook that clipped Prescott's chin and he went down for a six count. I could almost see the strength and resistance draining out of him as I stepped up my bombardment to the body. He gamely stood up to the best punches I could throw in the ninth round but it all took its toll in the tenth when I had him down for three and eight and wobbling all over the place as the bell rang.

Manager George Biddles summoned referee Frank Wilson and told him he was retiring the brave challenger despite Prescott's protests. It was a wise decision because Johnny had shifted a hell of a lot of punishment in the last three rounds and things could only have got worse. I couldn't believe it when his fickle fans jeered and booed Prescott and I gave them a rollocking on the MC's microphone. 'You should be cheering not booing,' I told them. 'Johnny's a game boy and has taken a lot of punishment.'

As I finished speaking it started hissing down with rain. If it had started half an hour earlier I'm not sure we would have got the fight finished. I reckon they might have had to throw a lifebelt in for 'young' Johnny!

The Aftermath

I don't think Prescott ever had his heart in the game to quite the same extent after I had destroyed his title ambitions. He gave more and more of his concentration to his bookmaking business and then switched his interests to scrap metal.

Defeats by Ray Patterson – Floyd's brother – and Argentinian Eduardo Corletti pushed him further down the heavyweight rankings. But then he had the chance to pull himself back into the championship picture when he fought his old friend and rival Jack Bodell at Wolverhampton in 1968. The fight was for the Midlands area championship and was featured on television.

There was a stunning start when Bodell had Prescott reeling on the ropes. But he was unable to finish it there and then and had to be satisfied with a points victory against an opponent who was as brave as they come. Prescott announced his retirement after his defeat but made a comeback 14 months later. He squashed 39 fights into his first four years as a professional, yet fought only ten more times in the next four years of his career. His two wars with Billy Walker followed by his punishing battle with me knocked a lot out of him and he was never quite the same force again.

He shares with Brian London and myself the despair of retiring after a defeat by Joe Bugner. Johnny bowed out after an eight-round points loss against Bugner at the Royal Albert Hall on 20 January 1970. It was an undistinguished end to a career that had promised so much more than it finally produced.

Johnny was a good-class boxer with a powerful jab and useful right; and he had plenty of heart and a charisma that would have made him a highly popular champion. What he lacked was the real gut commitment it takes to get to the top in boxing and stay there. I wonder just what he might have achieved had he been not quite so good looking and not so dedicated to having a good time as an unashamed playboy? Oh well, you can't have everything.

For the Record

Johnny Prescott

Born Birmingham, 20 August 1938.
Ht.: 6 ft. ½ in. Wt.: 13 st. 8 lb.
England amateur international.
Turned professional 1961. Managed by George Biddles.
Record: 50 fights, 34 wins, 4 draws, 12 losses (no KOs);
13 inside-the-distance wins (9 KOs).

10
The Fight: Muhammad Ali v. Henry Cooper
The Date: 21 May 1966
The Venue: Arsenal Football Stadium,
Highbury

The Build-up

Cassius Clay had changed his name to Muhammad Ali by the time we came to blows again on what was the most important fight night of my life. To be honest, I didn't care what he called himself as long as he was there to answer the first bell and give me a shot at his world title. The fact that I was also on a nice little earner was a bonus, but I would have fought for peanuts for a chance at getting my hands on *the* championship.

Clay's name – or rather Ali's – had become like poison to many people in the United States. He had publicly announced his allegiance to the Black Muslims and was refusing to be drafted into the US army for war duty in Vietnam because of his religious beliefs.

I admired his principles but struggled to understand his logic. By brilliant self-projection, showmanship in and out of the ring, and superb boxing skills, he had made the name Cassius Clay known throughout the world. Now he was disowning the identity because it had belonged to a white plantation boss who had enslaved his ancestors. I thought at the time that he had as much chance of becoming known and recognized as Muhammad Ali as I had of being called Shirley Temple. Everybody continued to refer to him as Cassius Clay in the build-up for our title fight. But it shows how wrong you can be because within a year or so he was universally known as Muhammad Ali and now, nearly 20 years on, I come across youngsters who think that Cassius Clay and Muhammad Ali are two different people.

Mind you, in a way I suppose they were because, although the Ali who filled Clay's boots had just as much to say for himself, a lot of the fun had gone out of him, and he was trying to convert people to his way of thinking with what amounted to sermons and hard-line political speeches. There were plenty of politicians and priests around to do that sort of thing and I didn't think the public wanted to hear it from their sports' heroes. Many cynics were doubting his sincerity but I'm sure he must have meant most of what he was saying because it was costing him an absolute fortune in lost commercial and endorsement contracts.

He had got himself heavily involved with 'Black Power' spokesman Michael X and later with Black Muslim leader Elijah Muhammad, whose son Herbert took over Ali's management after he had broken with the syndicate of white Kentucky businessmen who had handled him in his early years as a professional. In fact it was Michael X who made the first approach about staging a world title fight in Britain between Ali and I. My manager Jim Wicks gave him short shrift and told him that as far as he was concerned any promotion would be in the capable hands of Harry Levene, who had taken over from Jack Solomons as the leading British fight promoter.

Levene and his matchmaker Mickey Duff, along with the entrepreneurial backing of Jarvis Astaire who arranged world-wide closed-circuit television coverage of the fight, staged the most successful promotion in the history of British boxing. The contest was beamed live to cinemas in every major city in Britain apart from London. Ali was on a guaranteed £100,000 purse, plus considerable ancillary rights, such as North and South American closed-circuit and television, and a percentage on all TV, radio and film rights. I was on my best-ever pay day of a guaranteed £50,000 plus a percentage of the European and Far East TV and closed-circuit takings. It may not sound a fortune in these days when world champions can command millions of dollars, but, believe me, it was excellent take-home pay in that pre-decimalization era.

We attracted 45,000 spectators to Highbury – home of my favourite football team, Arsenal – and hundreds of thousands watched the fight on screens in places like Tokyo, Bangkok, Dortmund, Buenos Aires, Mexico City and Manchester.

Despite the spiteful Press treatment he had been getting in the United States, Ali received a rapturous welcome on his arrival in London. There was no doubting that his popularity was, if anything, on the increase outside his homeland and he commented: 'I've been driven out of my own country because of my religious beliefs, yet every other country in the world welcomes me. It's a strange feeling. All I ask is the same treatment and respect in my country that other boxers and athletes get from Uncle Sam.'

When it was pointed out to him that other American boxers and athletes were not refusing to join the US army, Clay replied: 'My religion is against war and I am within my legal rights to claim exemption on the basis of being a conscientious objector. If I weren't the heavyweight champion of the world there would be none of this fuss. While I'm here in Britain I don't want to be bothered with questions about my personal affairs, such as the draft case and my divorce. I'm here to defend my title and that old man Henry Cooper had better watch out. I'm feeling real mean.'

In the countdown to the fight, that memorable moment when I floored the then Cassius Clay with a left hook in the

fourth round at Wembley in 1963 must have been replayed on television and at cinemas more than a hundred times. While it helped sell tickets it worked against me in a way because every time it came on the screen or a photograph of the knockdown was shown in a newspaper it reminded Ali of the main danger to him. My left hook.

I knew this was going to make it that much harder to land what the media had dubbed 'Enery's 'Ammer. There was no way Ali was going to forget to duck because he was getting constant reminders of what could happen if he exposed his chin for just a split second, as he had at Wembley.

Since my victory over Johnny Prescott I had stupidly dropped a points decision to a spoiling fighter called Amos Johnson after he had floored me with a diabolical low blow that the referee didn't see. But that was just a silly off night and I later stopped two more Americans, Hubert Hilton and Jefferson Davis, in quick time to prove that the hammer was in good working order.

Ali had successfully twice defended the title following his farce of a fight against Sonny Liston in Maine. He had stopped former champion Floyd Patterson in 12 rounds in Las Vegas and he convincingly outpointed rough, tough Canadian George Chuvalo over 15 rounds in Toronto on 29 March 1966.

Both Ali and I showed we meant business by coming into the ring built for speed. Ali tipped the scales at 14 st. 3½ lb., which was the lightest he ever weighed as champion and 13 lb. less than when he had beaten Chuvalo just two months earlier. He had really got himself in shape, which I suppose was a compliment to me. I weighed in at 13 st. 4 lb. and felt as slim and as fit as a thoroughbred greyhound, without a surplus ounce on me. I knew I was going to need to be at my most mobile for this fight-night of my life.

The Fight

Ali had refused to sign the contract for the voluntary defence of his championship until promoter Harry Levene promised to provide a largest-possible 20 ft. ring. Harry had to have one specially made at a cost of 500 quid. It was a crafty move by the champion. He wanted as much room in which to manoeuvre as possible. Years earlier, when Don Cockell challenged for the world title, Rocky Marciano had demanded a postage-stamp size 16 ft. ring. The harder the punch you carry the smaller the ring you require because it means you can get to your opponent quicker. Ali had chosen a ring in which we could have had a football match. The left hook I had landed back in 1963 obviously left a permanent mark on his memory and he wanted as much room as possible in which to take evasive action.

The last thing I did before the main floodlights were turned off was to wave to my wife Albina who, for the one and only time in my career, was in a ringside seat watching me fight. She hated every moment of it and hardly appreciated that the big fight atmosphere was the most electric and exciting that I had ever experienced.

It was quickly obvious what tactics Ali was going to adopt. He was wheeling and circling in the ballroom-size ring towards my left side, preventing me getting a full swing with the hook. We fell into an early clinch and as I tried to work away with both hands he grabbed me and held my arms so tightly I felt as if I was in the grip of a vice.

Every time I got near him all he did was catch hold of me as if I were an unwilling dancing partner, and he kept as firm a hold as he could until the referee said 'Break'. Then, worried that I might hit him on the break, he pushed me hard and jumped back out of distance. This is how he continually reacted the moment I got close enough to threaten any real damage. After a couple of rounds sussing out just what Ali was up to, I started to try similar tactics, holding him with

my right and firing off lefts to the head and ribs but with
little success.

We knew he'd be watching for the left hook, so during my
training sessions I had practised the right hand a lot more
although throughout my career I had never been really effec-
tive with it. My plan was to try to kid Ali with a few rights
which would make him forget the left hook, so I didn't try to
throw too many in the first round.

I was aiming to match the champion jab for jab, but in
the first round I was short with the left. Most of my punches
were falling an inch or two short as Ali skipped and danced
his way round and round the massive ring surface. But as I
hadn't warmed up, I wasn't too concerned. Ali was keeping
on the move, retreating behind a stabbing left that carried
little weight but which stopped me setting myself for any big
punches. I was doing all the forcing but he was keeping that
left in my face and I reckon we were about level on points at
the end of the round. Neither of us landed a really telling
blow in that first round, and as I returned to my corner I
knew I was going to find it harder than ever getting my
favourite punch home. Ali was determined not to allow a
repeat of 1963.

The pattern of the fight was set in that first round, and
rounds two and three were a carbon copy, with the one
difference that I managed to hurt Ali with a solid left hook
in the third. But he smothered my attempts at a follow-up
and was soon back on his rhythmic, retreating circular tour
of the ring, making me miss with clever footwork and crafty
feints.

Ali was a much-improved fighter since our previous
meeting in 1963. He had learnt a lot about how to look after
himself inside, and while not causing any damage himself was
very adept at tying me up with illegal holding on the blindside
of referee George Smith. We were both getting away with 'old
pro' tricks.

Ali came down a gear in the fourth round and I started to

reach him. I was getting home with some good, solid left leads but could not pin him with the all-important left hook. Once or twice the hook missed him by a whisker. During the fourth round Ali protested to the referee, not for hitting on the break, as some ringsiders thought, but for a low blow. Some people said afterwards, 'Why didn't you go in and belt him while he was having a moan?' But he was two or three yards out of distance. Directly I went for him he composed himself, and started backing away behind that long, snaking left jab.

There wasn't much between us again in the fifth round. We were scoring a jab for a jab but I was feeling good and knew I still had a lot to give. At 32 I was giving nine years to the champion, but I was as fit as I had ever been in my life and felt I could come on strong because I was sure there was no way Ali could keep up the blinding pace at which he was circling the ring.

I thought to myself that once he started slowing I would concentrate on releasing my heaviest punches. Then came the sixth round and the most disappointing and most frustrating moment of my life.

We had been boxing at long range for about half a minute when he caught me as we both moved forward to launch punches, and as he moved away from me I felt blood oozing from a cut over my left eye. Immediately after the fight I told the ringside reporters that there was a clash of heads. I was not accusing the champion of doing it deliberately. He never was that type of dirty fighter. But my honest opinion was that the injury had been caused by his head. That was how it felt at the time. Ali threw a right hand as I was coming in and something hard hit me. In the heat of the battle I thought it was his head. Afterwards, looking at the film, I could see I had made a mistake and I have since apologized to Ali for arriving at the wrong conclusion. He threw a left and a right, and as he threw the right I also slung a punch. He shortened his right as I came forward and the effect was a chopping

blow on my eye with the heel of his glove. The eye split wide.
open. It was the worst cut I ever had in boxing, deeper and
longer even than in my first fight with him. It was in the
moment immediately after his right landed that our heads
came together, which made me think at the time that the
damage was done by a butt. The cheers of the crowd turned
into a long, audible gasp that gradually changed tone into a
deep-throated groan.

Nobody had to tell me it was a bad cut. I knew at once
that I was in desperate trouble. I could feel the warm blood
gushing down my face and onto my shoulders and chest; it
was really blinding me. Ali said afterwards that because of
his religious beliefs he didn't want to cause me any more
damage, but if you ever see the film you will notice that he
pounced like a panther, landing as many punches on the cut
as he could.

Referee George Smith looked at the cut once and then
allowed me to box on. I knew I was fighting on borrowed
time and I went almost berserk, throwing left hooks in an
uncharacteristically wild bid to land a knock-out blow.
Usually I was in control of myself in the boxing ring, but this
was one occasion when I just put my head down and started
swinging. But my vision was badly impaired and Ali easily
avoided my reckless punches, and when he landed several
long-range pot shots of his own right on the eye the referee
had no option but to stop what had become a bloodbath after
one minute 38 seconds of the sixth round.

As in our first fight, I was left wondering about what might
have been. Most judges had me either all square or just ahead
on points at the end and I knew I still had plenty in reserve.
In 11 rounds of boxing Ali had never once had me in serious
trouble apart from the cuts. I'd had him down once and had
won more rounds that I had lost.

I just wish I could have battled against him without the
cut-eye curse. But what's the point in wasting time and print
on hypothetical theories? The fact is that Muhammad Ali,

Cassius Clay that was, had retained the world championship. The dream I had harboured since I was a kid, pretending to be Joe Louis, remained just that. A dream.

The Aftermath

I could have wept with frustration when I returned to the Arsenal home dressing-room and the equally disappointed Jim Wicks kept the press boys away from me for a while so that I could compose myself. In the visitors' dressing-room along the corridor Ali was holding court and told reporters: 'Henry hurt me just once. It was a left hook in the third round. But I was too fast for him tonight. He couldn't catch me again. I opened the cut with a left-right combination. I wanted the referee to stop it straight away. The blood disturbed me a lot. It was pure violence, and that was against my personal feelings and my religion. Henry's a good fighter but his flesh is weak. If the fight had not been stopped I am confident I would have knocked him out in the ninth or tenth round. You see, gentlemen, I am the Greatest.'

I made my accusation in the dressing-room that the cut had been caused by Ali's head. But I put the record straight the moment I studied the fight on film. I told the reporters that I hadn't done badly 'for an old bum and a cripple'. This is what Ali had called me before the fight as part of his sales pitch.

There was a lot of conjecture in the newspapers and on television and radio about whether I should retire. Ali was drawn into it and said something about me being what we call in the trade a 'bleeder'. He thought along with most people that the time had come for me to call it a day. I went and had plastic surgery on the eye injury and quietly thought about my future. After careful consideration I decided there was still plenty I could achieve in the game – and I hung around for another four and a half years!

Ali returned to London later in that summer of 1966 and polished off Brian London in three rounds at Earls Court, and then the following month stopped off in Frankfurt to put down a brave challenge by European champion Karl Mildenberger in the 12th round.

He then returned home to the United States to try to convince his countrymen that Cassius Clay was no more. Clay was dead. Long live Ali!

11

The Fight: Muhammad Ali v. Ernie Terrell
The Date: 6 February 1967
The Venue: Houston Astrodome, Texas

The Build-up

About the time that Clay and Liston were preparing for their second 'fight' the World Boxing Association announced that they were stripping Clay of the world championship because he had entered into a return-match agreement with Liston. They nominated Ernie Terrell and Eddie Machen to fight for their version of the title and Terrell was proclaimed as the new champion after outpointing Machen in Chicago on 5 March 1965.

So suddenly we had two world heavyweight champions – Cassius Clay, recognized by the World Boxing Council, and Ernie Terrell, holder of the WBA title. It was inevitable that they would be matched in a summit showdown and after nearly two years of political in-fighting they were finally brought face to face in the space-age setting of the $45 million Houston Astrodome – 'an astronomical stadium for an astronomical fight' as the promotion publicists put it.

Terrell, a 6 ft. 6 in. giant from Chicago via Mississippi, had an impressive ring record. He had won 39 of 43 contests since turning professional in 1957 and was on a winning streak of 15 successive victories against top-quality opposition since avenging a defeat by Cleveland Williams in 1962.

He was a stand-up boxer with a high guard and a powerful jab. There was no dynamite in his gloves but his punches were solid and most of his opponents had found him a difficult man to hit because of his 84-inch reach. In two defences of the WBA title Terrell had proved himself a commanding ring general with points victories over George Chuvalo and Doug Jones, both of whom had gone the distance with Ali and given him a tough time.

Terrell's was the classic rags-to-riches story. Born on 4 April 1939, he was the sixth oldest of ten children of a poor Mississippi farmer who moved his family to a black ghetto on Chicago's tough South Side. Ernie learned to look after himself in Chicago's mean streets and was so useful with his fists that he was talked into becoming an amateur boxer.

The hardest job they had was finding him matches against boys his own age because at 14 he measured 6 ft. 4in. and weighed just a couple of pounds under 14 stone. At 16 he won the novice class in the Golden Gloves competition and turned professional two years later after impressive victories for Chicago in inter-city matches.

He was spotted by millionaire sports fanatic George Hamid, who signed him up on a contract that guaranteed Terrell a generous 85 per cent of all profits from a company formed in his name. The company was not only projecting Ernie as a boxer but also as a guitar-playing singer, and he toured the United States with his backing group, the Heavyweights, which included in the line-up two of his brothers and a sister.

There was genuinely no love lost between Terrell and Ali. The spiteful things they were saying about each other before the fight were not, as is usual, to attract an audience. In the United States at least, Ali had still not got his wish to be

recognized as Muhammad Ali. Most people over there continued to call him Clay. Prominent among them was Ernie Terrell, a fellow black whom Ali insulted by describing him as an 'Uncle Tom' – that is a downtrodden black person who is servile and in the keep of white men. Ali always poured scorn on his opponents but a lot of his insults were delivered with tongue in cheek to help boost ticket sales. With Terrell it was different. Ali meant every word. He could not forgive him for refusing to refer to him as Muhammad Ali.

'I feel real malice towards Clay,' Terrell told reporters. 'You have all built him up as some sort of superman but he ain't nothing special. He's just another fighter with two hands. After I've knocked him out to prove that I'm the real number one, I will not want to socialize with him. I usually get on well with my opponents after we've fought. But it'll be different with Clay. I just don't like the man.' It was all very nasty and Ali countered with some verbal violence of his own. 'I'm going to ask Terrell just one question at the weigh-in,' he said. 'I'll just quietly ask him what my name is. If he gives the wrong answer I'll give him the torture treatment. I'll be talking and punching, making him miss and then doing some more talking and punching until the referee has to save him. I won't give him the easy way out of a knock-out. I'm going to hurt him real bad if he doesn't give me the right anwer to my question. If he gives the right answer, I'll show mercy and knock him out early.'

It was odd to hear Ali talking about a knock-out because he was never recognized as a one-punch finisher, even taking into account his first-round victory over Sonny Liston. However, there had been evidence that he was developing heavier punching power three months earlier when he stopped Cleveland 'Big Cat' Williams in three rounds after flooring him four times. Now he was promising to give Terrell a hiding if he failed to come up with the right answer to his question.

JOE LOUIS v. JERSEY JOE WALCOTT
My boyhood idol, Joe Louis (left), scores with a left to the body and looks at an inviting target around challenger Jersey Joe Walcott's rib section

BRUCE WOODCOCK v. FREDDIE MILLS
It's the calm before the storm as Bruce Woodcock (left) and Freddie Mills spar at long range. Bruce later got to work with his mighty right and knocked out big-hearted Freddie in the fourteenth round

*ROCKY MARCIANO
v. DON COCKELL*
*This right under the
heart was one of the
hundreds of blows
that brave Don Cockell
shifted against rough,
tough Rocky Marciano
(right) before the
referee came to his
rescue*

INGEMAR JOHANSSON v. FLOYD PATTERSON
*Ingo's Bingo floors Floyd Patterson for the seventh time and Ingemar
Johansson takes over as the first European holder of the world title since
Max Schmeling*

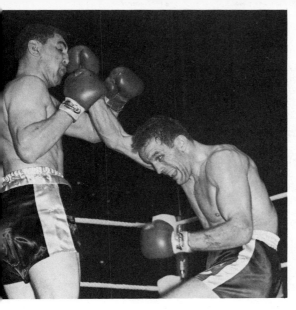

HENRY COOPER v.
JOE ERSKINE
*I'm taking a right liberty
here with Joe Erskine's
hooter when he was
expecting a body attack.
This was the fight in
which I feared I had
broken Joe's back when
he went through the
ropes in the twelfth
round*

HENRY COOPER v. BRIAN LONDON
*And they said I couldn't use my right!
Here's photographic evidence that I
could whack with my right hand. Brian
London is on the receiving end and I'm
on my way to the British title*

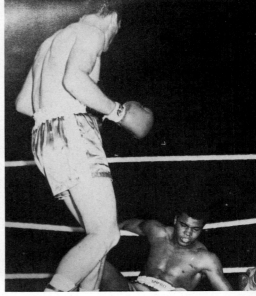

HENRY COOPER v. CASSIUS CLAY
*My favourite picture. Cassius Clay as
he then was has just taken my left
hook on his chops. The bell rang
seconds later and my chances of
winning went with it*

SONNY LISTON v. FLOYD PATTERSON
Awesome Sonny Liston (right) delivers the final left hook that flattened
Floyd Patterson and gave the world a controversial new champion. "We
wouldn't even want to meet that geezer Liston walking down the street,"
said my lovely old manager Jim Wicks

MUHAMMAD ALI v. SONNY LISTON
There was conjecture that this third-round punch from Muhammad Ali
(left) caused the shoulder injury that forced Sonny Liston's shock
retirement at the end of the sixth round. I reckon Old Stoneface was
suffering more from a broken spirit

HENRY COOPER v. JOHNNY PRESCOTT
I was happy to let Johnny Prescott lead like this in our British title fight so that I could counter with hooks to the body that finally forced the game Midlander's surrender

MUHAMMAD ALI v. ERNIE TERRELL
This was Muhammad Ali at his meanest, demanding that Ernie Terrell (left) should tell him his name while handing him a painful hiding

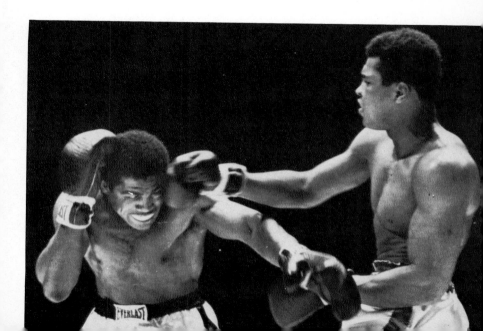

HENRY COOPER v. JOSE URTAIN
Jose Urtain (right) was built like a brick outhouse but big muscles mean nothing in boxing. It's the timing of your punches that matter and I found it easy to avoid the Spaniard's feared right handers

JOE FRAZIER v. MUHAMMAD ALI
This is the left hook that clinched Joe Frazier's points victory against Muhammad Ali in their 'Fight of the Century.' It dropped Ali in the fifteenth and final round and it was a wonder he managed to get up and finish the fight on his feet.

HENRY COOPER v. BILLY WALKER
I used my left hand like a trombone slide against Billy Walker (right) and retained my British title with an eighth-round stoppage. The victory earned me a third Lonsdale Belt outright

MUHAMMAD ALI v. GEORGE FOREMAN George Foreman (left) is on his way down and out as Muhammad Ali regains the world heavyweight championship with an eighth-round knockout in Zaire

JOE BUGNER v. HENRY COOPER I'm out of distance with an intended left jab against Joe Bugner (left) on the night of my last fight but I was convinced I had landed enough punches to have won the contest. Referee Harry Gibbs thought otherwise

MUHAMMAD ALI v. LEON SPINKS
Leon Spinks (right) seems to be bowing to Muhammad Ali's supremacy as
'The Greatest' adds to his legend by becoming the first man to regain the
world heavyweight title for a second time

MUHAMMAD ALI v. LARRY HOLMES
One of the saddest sights in boxing. Muhammad Ali is forced to quit on his
stool at the end of the tenth round of his world championship battle with
the new hero Larry Holmes

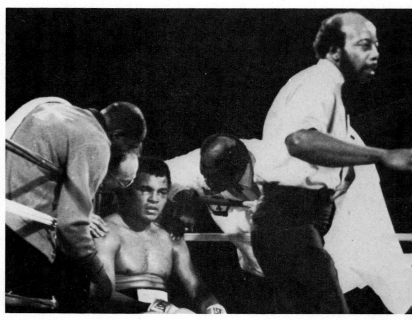

The Fight

Ali was true to his word, although he didn't ask the question at the weigh-in where Terrell openly referred to him as Cassius Clay. He saved it for when they got into the ring in front of a world record indoor attendance of 37,321 at the Houston Astrodome, a magnificent sports stadium described in that quaint style of understatement that Americans have as being 'the eighth wonder of the world'.

While the referee was giving his pre-fight instructions, Ali pushed his face in front of Terrell's and asked: 'What's my name?' He kept repeating the question until a perspiring Terrell pushed him angrily away. You could have cut the tension with a knife as the first bell rang.

Ali, as everybody had come to realize, was a man of many moods and many faces. He showed the ugly side of his nature against Terrell. In the opening five rounds he seemed as much interested in talking as fighting and with almost every other punch that he threw he asked: 'What's my name?'

It was fairly even in the first third of the fight but from the sixth round Ali started to get right on top and punished Terrell with a stream of punches to the head that opened cuts around both eyes. This was Ali at his most cocky and arrogant and he continually snarled and taunted, and on one sickening occasion spat contemptuously at the feet of his outclassed opponent.

He was not only hammering Terrell but humiliating him as well, yet at the same time demeaning himself with sportsmanship that slipped to gutter level. Terrell was not the only loser that night. Boxing also took a bashing because of Ali's unforgivable behaviour. I was always a Muhammad Ali fan but in this fight he stretched my allegiance almost to breaking point.

An uppercut followed by a two-fisted combination of straight punches to the head had Terrell draped over the ropes in the seventh round, and a whiplash left hook almost lifted him off his feet in the eighth. Both men were guilty of frequent fouls that would have got them thrown out of the ring in most countries. Several times I noticed Ali pulling the old pro's trick of rubbing his thumb across Terrell's eye and he used the sort of armlock tactics inside with which he had frustrated me in our second battle. Terrell in turn was guilty of wrestling and landing kidney punches and low blows, but Ali treated them with disdain and just stepped up what he so aptly described as his torture treatment.

It wasn't pretty to watch and the only thing you could admire was Terrell's courage in standing up to a non-stop barrage of punches as Ali treated him as if he were a human punchbag.

In previous fights, Ali had been showing off his 'Ali shuffle' footwork tricks and his 'float like a butterfly, sting like a bee' ring technique. But against Terrell there was no clowning or showmanship. He displayed as much humour and compassion as an assassin and just concentrated on hurting and ridiculing his opponent. Terrell revealed later that Ali was not only demanding to be told his name but was saying: 'You're an Uncle Tom negro and you're going to get messed up.'

Ali finished a runaway points winner. Referee Harry Kessler scored it 148–137, judge Ernie Taylor 148–137 and judge Jimmy Webb 148–133 – all in favour of Ali. If they had been fighting in Britain the referee would have stopped it long before the end because Terrell was so far behind on points. And any British referee would have told Ali very early in the fight: 'Cut out the talking. You're here to fight not to talk.'

It was all brutal, bloody, squalid stuff. And boxing, as well as Terrell, was the loser.

The Aftermath

Terrell took such a hammering from Ali that it was six months before he could fight again. He was just a shell of the fighter who had won the WBA version of the world crown and after points defeats by Eddie Machen and a mediocre Mexican heavyweight called Manuel Ramos he announced his retirement. Three years later Terrell made an indifferent comeback and finally packed the game in for good after a one-round drubbing from young heavyweight prospect Jeff Merritt in 1973.

Clay knew he was fighting on borrowed time. He was squashing in as many title defences as possible before he took on his biggest opponent – a Federal Grand Jury. Just six weeks after his destruction of Terrell he put his title on the line against Zora Folley in New York and won by a seventh-round knockout. It was to be his last fight for three years and seven months.

On 9 May 1967, Clay was stripped of his world championship following an indictment by a Federal Grand Jury in Houston for refusing to serve in the US armed forces on religious grounds. He was banned from boxing in the United States and had his passport confiscated.

While Ali was on the sidelines fighting legal battles to keep out of jail, the World Boxing Association and New York State held a series of eliminators to find his successor as champion. All major boxing bodies finally recognized Joe Frazier as the undisputed king after he had stopped Jimmy Ellis in four rounds in New York on 16 February 1970.

Eight months later the former champion – by then recognized even in the United States as Muhammad Ali – started his comeback at the age of 28. He returned to the ring in the Deep South in Atlanta and was well in command against Jerry Quarry when a thumping right hand opened a cut over Quarry's eye, forcing him to retire at the end of the third round.

Then, on 7 December 1970, Ali was coasting to a comfortable points victory against Oscar Bonavena when he suddenly turned on his full power and forced the referee's intervention in the 15th and last round to save the Argentinian from further punishment.

'Now I want Frazier,' said Ali, who was describing himself as 'The People's Champion'. 'That man has got *my* title.'

We'll take our ringside seats for the classic Frazier–Ali 'Fight of the Century' in a couple of chapters time.

For the Record

Ernie Terrell

Born Inverness, Mississippi, 4 April 1939.
Ht.: 6 ft. 6 in. Wt.: 15 st. 4 lb.
Turned professional 1957. Managed by George Hamid.
Honours: WBA heavyweight champion 1965–7.
Record: 54 fights, 45 wins, 9 losses (no KOs); 21 inside-the-distance wins (6 KOs).

12
The Fight: Henry Cooper v. Billy Walker
The Date: 7 November 1967
The Venue: Wembley Arena

The Build-up

Billy Walker was, to use an East Endism, 'as game as a beigel'. Those many mimics who do me the honour of impersonating me always use my old line, 'He's a good strong boy.' That really sums up Billy, who never minded taking two, three or four punches to get in one of his own. He fought with his face a bit too much for my taste, but there was no denying that his biff-bang-wallop style won him many fans.

They dubbed him the 'Golden Boy' of British boxing and there was nobody to touch him as a ticket-seller. His name on the bill almost guaranteed a sell-out at any London venue. He was brilliantly guided by his brother George, who invested all the money they earned with such vision that he has since become a highly successful City tycoon and respected film producer.

The youngest of three sons of a Stepney brewery drayman, Billy followed big brother George into the boxing game. George was ABA light-heavyweight champion in 1951, the year before I won the title for the first time. He was a classy professional and in March 1953 fought Welshman Dennis Powell at Liverpool Stadium for the vacant British cruiserweight crown. It was one of the bloodiest battles in British boxing history and George was forced to retire after 11 brutal rounds. When he returned home, he had to stay indoors for a week nursing his injuries, which included a lip that was so badly gashed he had to drink everything through a straw.

Young Billy was then just 14 and he stayed away from school to keep George company. The state of his brother had a big effect on him and he swore that he'd never have anything to do with the fight game. Five years later, shortly after his 19th birthday, Billy started to attend the West Ham amateur gymnasium for fitness training. He slipped the gloves on for a sparring session with a partner who towered over him. George was looking on as Billy threw a right that knocked the big feller spark out. From then on George encouraged Billy to take his boxing seriously and he started to go from strength to strength.

As an amateur Billy won 26 of 33 contests and had a great year in 1961 when he stopped 15 out of 17 opponents, including 13 clean knock-outs. There was no doubt that he could bang; and as well as punching power he also had a strong chin.

His biggest stroke of luck came in the famous amateur international match when England whitewashed the United States ten-nil. Billy, who was the ABA heavyweight champion, was last into the ring. The United States were represented by a giant of a guy called Cornelius Perry, who was the fattest heavyweight I have ever seen. Billy knocked him cold in the first round and millions of television viewers saw his spectacular win.

Billy was the talk of Britain the next day, a real overnight star, and George cleverly cashed in on his popularity by negotiating a deal with promoter Harry Levene for Billy's first three professional fights at what was reported as a record pay out of £9,000.

It was great for his bank balance but I don't think it did him any real favours as far as his boxing career was concerned. He went straight into the eight-round class and did not have the benefit of learning his trade the way he needed to.

Along with everybody else, I liked Billy. He was a smashing bloke with a lot of charisma. Advertisers also liked him and he had a glamour image that brought him endorsement contracts for things like clothes and hair dressing. But at the end of the day it was for his performances in the ring that he was going to be judged and, frankly, I didn't think he was in my league. I hope that doesn't sound too arrogant, but you need confidence to be the guv'nor in boxing and I was convinced I would always have the beating of Billy.

My manager Jim Wicks and I watched his progress with close interest because we knew it could mean a big pay day if he got into championship class. Two Londoners, two heavy-weights, two big-punch specialists, and both of us with a big following from our own manors. That could only add up to a lot of money at the box-office. Jim used to rub his hands and say: 'That boy is made for us. We can beat him with one arm tied behind our back.' I felt almost as confident!

The Walker camp had been making noises about fighting me since Billy had outpointed my old rival Joe Erskine over ten rounds in his 17th fight on 27 October 1964. Billy – or was it his ghostwriter? – went into print with the statement: 'I'm now ready for Henry Cooper. He's past 30 and an old man in boxing terms. It's not good for the game to have a champion reigning for too long. It's time we had a young champion. I'm ready to meet Henry just as soon as somebody puts up the lolly.' I had heard all this sort of thing before from Johnny Prescott and had put him in his place. I was looking forward to giving Billy the same treatment, but he suffered a painful points defeat by Brian London followed by a draw and then a defeat against Argentinian Eduardo Corletti. It meant a shelving of plans to bring us together in the 'Battle of London'.

Billy started to get back on the winning trail with a run of six victories against some pretty undistinguished opposition. He got off the canvas to score a good eighth-round win over Ray Patterson, Floyd's brother, and then put up a game performance in a European title challenge against Karl Mildenberger on 21 March 1967, before being stopped with a cut eye in the eighth round.

Three months later I stopped that awkward cuss of a southpaw Jack Bodell in two rounds for a seventh successful defence of my British championship. Billy Walker was next on the agenda. We would soon see who was 'King of the Cockneys'.

The Fight

My plan for the fight with Billy was to soften him up with left jabs for the first half of the contest and then open up with my heaviest artillery from about the seventh round. I had used similar tactics against Johnny Prescott with good effect. Walker and Prescott had knocked hell out of each other in two back-to-back battles in 1963 and I don't think either of them was ever quite the same force after they had severely punished each other. Johnny was the better boxer, but Billy was the more dangerous puncher and could really take a whack on the jaw. I knew it was pointless trying to knock him out early. I just might have knocked up my hands trying to finish him, so I concentrated on boxing him and making sure I didn't get caught napping by one of his haymakers.

The trouble with Billy was you could see his big right-hand punch coming a mile away. He used to telegraph it and it was easy to step inside or block it, and to counter with a left to his unguarded head.

Everything went perfectly to plan. I kept pumping out the old trombone left and Billy kept eating it up. His defence was all over the place and every time he set himself for one of his roundhouse rights I just knocked him off balance with a left lead.

I have to give Billy credit for never giving up and he was always trying to land the big one that could swing the fight his way, but there was hardly a moment when I didn't feel as if I was in complete command of the proceedings.

A lot of the newspaper experts had predicted that Billy would cut me up with his rough, tough tactics but, ironically, it was the East Ender who suffered a bad injury. I opened an inch-long slit over his eye and it was obvious in the seventh round that he was struggling.

During the interval at the end of the round, Jim Wicks said: 'You know what you've got to do.' He didn't have to add anthing else. I'd been in the pro game a long time and could be coldly devastating when I had to be. I piled a procession of at least 30 punches into his face without reply in the eighth round. It was the most one-sided round of boxing I had ever experienced. He just had no idea how to get out of the way of my punches. Billy was close to exhaustion and I was making the cut my target. I know that sounds horrible but it's a tough old game and I was doing exactly what Muhammad Ali did to me in our two fights.

The referee stopped it late in the eighth with Billy, as brave as always, looking a mess. He hadn't given me much trouble and the victory meant I had won a third Lonsdale Belt outright, a record for the British heavyweight division.

The Aftermath

It was funny reading reports of the fight in which Billy Walker was being advised to retire. It was me they had been telling to jack it in the previous year after my defeat by Ali.

Billy was five years younger than me but the reckless way he fought meant there was no way he could have a long career in the game. In fact, he had just two more fights after our battle. Following a year lay-off he returned to the ring on 12 November 1968, and produced one of the most impressive performances of his career when he thumped high-ranking American Thad Spencer to a six-round defeat.

Billy was the darling of the fans again but talk of him getting back into championship reckoning was silenced at Wembley on 25 March 1969. He was dropped for a count of eight in the first round of a vicious duel with Swadlincote southpaw Jack Bodell. Billy was on the verge of a knock-out defeat but survived the round and came battling back after taking another count in the second round. In round five it was Bodell's turn to visit the canvas and he only just beat the ten-second count. But Billy was by then fighting on courage alone and Bodell gave him a terrible hiding over the next three rounds before the referee stopped it in the eighth after the West Ham idol had taken another count of eight.

It was the last time we saw Billy in the ring. He retired to Jersey to live on the profits he had earned the hard way while George Walker continued to build a business empire, using brain instead of brawn. Few boxers have ever given value for money like Billy did. But a fighting heart will take you only so far. Billy, the Golden Boy, just didn't have the necessary skill and technique to back his bravery.

For the Record

Billy Walker

Born Stepney, 3 March 1939.
Ht.: 6 ft. Wt.: 14 st.
ABA heavyweight champion 1961
Turned professional 1961. Managed by brother George Walker.

Record: 31 fights, 21 wins, 2 draws, 8 losses (no KOs); 18 inside-the-distance wins (7 KOs).

13

The Fight: Henry Cooper v. Jose Urtain
The Date: 10 November 1970
The Venue: Wembley Arena

The Build-up

I had a funny old on-off affair with the European championship. I won the title on three separate occasions, had it taken
away once, gave it up once and finally had it nicked off me
by Joe Bugner.

To be honest, the championship was often more of a burden
than a bonus. The moment you won it you became the puppet
of the European Boxing Union. They dictated who you had
to defend against and where and when. If you didn't jump –
or fight – when they wanted you to they'd have the title off
you quicker than you could say Sugar Ray Robinson.

I first won the title in 1964 after Ingemar Johansson's
retirement had left the championship vacant. Brian London
and I were the top two contenders and I beat him on points
over 15 rounds at Belle Vue, Manchester.

That was when I found I had an opponent outside the ring
who was more stubborn than any I had ever met inside the
ropes: the European Boxing Union. I was all set to defend

against German southpaw Karl Mildenberger, the official No.
1 contender. Ideally I would liked to have fought him in
Britain but those were the days when there was still some
anti-German feeling about and as our major promoters were
Jewish there was no way they were going to be seen lining a
German boxer's pockets. So, reluctantly, I agreed to go to
Germany to defend the title after the fight had been put out
to purse offers by the EBU.

When I started training for the contest I felt a recurrence
of the arthritic-type pain that I often suffered in my left elbow.
Two specialists told me I needed to rest it for two weeks. The
German promoter was suspicious to the point of disbelieving
and so we summoned him and an EBU representative to
London and showed them X-rays and the specialist reports.
The promoter reacted by saying he would postpone the fight
for two weeks, which was useless to me because I would be
losing two weeks training.

He said it was the only date he had and so Jim Wicks told
him: 'Let's forget it then, because we won't be ready.' The
next we knew the EBU had stripped me of the title and
nominated Mildenberger to fight for the suddenly vacant
championship against a mediocre Italian called Sante Amonti
who was knocked out in one round in Berlin. Not so long
afterwards Mildenberger was injured when due to defend the
title and he was given a month's grace to get fit. So you can
imagine why we were fighting mad with the inconsistent
EBU.

Mildenberger was still champion when I next challenged
for the title that I had lost without throwing a punch. Harry
Levene buried his anti-German feelings and brought Mildenberger over to fight me at Wembley on 18 September 1968 –
my only fight that year because of trouble with a dodgy knee.

'I don't like paying this Kraut,' said Harry, 'but at least
I know I'll have the satisfaction of seeing you give him a
hiding.'

Mildenberger was a thick-set all-rounder who could box a

bit and bang a bit as the occasion demanded. He had given Ali a tough time before being stopped in the 12th round of a world title fight in September 1966. A victory over me would have given him a record seven successful defences of the European title. As it turned out I gave him a bit of a pasting for eight rounds, dictating the pattern of the fight with my left hand that was never out of his face. He got really frustrated at not being able to land any of his big bombs and started to get reckless with his head. One diabolical butt in the eighth round opened a cut over my right eye and the referee had no option but to disqualify the German.

Six months later I defended the title against an Italian wild man of the ring called Piero Tomasoni, who was fittingly nicknamed 'The Axeman' because he used to swing his punches as if trying to chop down a tree.

We fought in Rome on 13 March 1969 – and it was nearly an unlucky 13th for me. Tomasoni went berserk after I had floored him in the first round. He was throwing punches from all angles and he didn't care where they landed. One right hand in the second round whacked me so low that it dented my aluminium foul cup. If I had not been wearing the protection I reckon I would have been writing this book as Ms Henrietta Cooper! I went down on my knees with my eyes watering and couldn't believe it when Dutch referee Ben Bril started to count over me. Tomasoni should have been thrown out of the ring there and then.

I pulled myself up and started to unload my heaviest punches on an opponent who was as dangerous as a wild bull. I had him over in the fourth round and as he fell he pulled me down with him. As I got up he thumped in another low blow. The referee at last warned him and this was the signal for the fanatical Roman crowd to launch fruit, bread rolls and salami into the ring. I could have fed myself for a week on what came pelting out of the crowd. They obviously don't have hungry fighters in Italy!

Blimey, I thought to myself, I'd better get this over quick

because it'll be their seats being thrown in next. I finally ended Tomasoni's all-or-nothing challenge in the fifth round with a left hook that sent him slumping to the canvas. I was one helluva relieved champion when he just failed to beat the count.

By the end of the year I was a champion without a title to my name. I gave up my British and Empire crowns in protest at the British Boxing Board of Control's stinking decision not to recognize a proposed fight with American Jimmy Ellis as being for the world championship. I have never been so upset in my life as with the Board on that issue. You'd have thought they would have bent over backwards to see a British champion getting a crack at the title, but they vetoed it because they were supporters of the New York version of the title rather than the WBA championship. I knew in my heart that it was only the equivalent of half a world title, but half a loaf is better than none . . . and I would have earned a nice crust against a boxer I was confident I could have beaten.

I had held the British and Empire titles since 1959 and had won a record three Lonsdale Belts outright. We, Jim Wicks and I, reckoned the Board had treated us disgracefully after all the money they had earned out of my purses. The one time in my career when I needed their support and they were suddenly the invisible men. We gave up the hard-earned titles to emphasize our disgust and then started to train for an unsanctioned world title fight with Ellis in either Rome or Dublin.

Then my old knee trouble came back to plague me and all plans were shelved while I went into hospital for a cartilage operation. This meant I also had to surrender my European crown because there was no way the EBU was going to be compassionate and wait for me to make a full recovery.

A lot of people wrote the 'old man' off as finished, but after training harder than I'd ever done in my life with my favourite Arsenal footballers I was fit and raring to go again; and on 24 March 1970 I regained my British and Empire titles by outpointing clumsy yet dangerous southpaw Jack Bodell over 15 hard but fairly pedestrian rounds at Wembley Arena.

This has all been a long-winded way of bringing me to one of my most satisfactory fights – against Spaniard Jose Urtain, who had taken over as European champion on 3 April 1970 by knocking out Germany's Peter Wieland in seven rounds in Madrid. He had won 33 of his 35 fights inside the distance and his only defeat was on a disqualification; 30 of his opponents had not got past the third round.

I have never known anybody in the fight game quite like Urtain. He came from the Basque country around San Sebastian and was a champion rock lifter. The Urtain family are folk heroes in the Basque territitory of north-east Spain. Jose followed a long line of Urtains who were legendary for their feats of strength. His grandfather was at one time reputed to be the strongest man in the world and Jose was considered in that league because of the weight of rock he could lift with his bare hands.

Sheer strength does not necessarily mean you can fight, but Jose had a reputation as a wicked puncher. They reckoned that if he landed with his mighty right hand the recipient wouldn't know anything about it until he woke up some minutes later. But when I studied Urtain's record I found I'd heard of hardly any of the opponents he'd been knocking over. I felt sure he had got to the top on the back of a bum-of-the-month campaign. Promoter Harry Levene had to pay him a small fortune to get him to agree to defend his European title against me at Wembley, and what with his reputation as a banger and the fact that at 27 he was nine years my junior there were not too many punters who fancied my chances when I climbed into the ring to try to win the European crown for a third time.

The Fight

I spent the first round feeling Urtain out. He was stocky and built like a brick out-house, with wide shoulders that went on for ever and brawny, muscular arms that showed all the evidence of his rock-lifting pastime. He was quickly swinging that right of his but in such crude fashion that I was soon thinking to myself: 'Take your time, Henry. You've got a right mug here. Just don't do anything silly.'

I set about giving him a boxing lesson, stabbing long left leads into his face and moving inside his swings that were so obvious that he might just as well have sent me a postcard to say they were coming. The only real problem he gave me was with his head, which was bouncing dangerously in front of my face everytime we went into a clinch. I picked up a cut in the first round but Eddie Thomas, who had taken over in the corner from my long-time trainer Danny Holland, did a superb repair job and I was not unduly worried by it.

Urtain was tiring himself out, throwing big right handers that were putting ringside spectators in more danger than me. As he began to slow I stepped up my pace and started to double up with the left jab and then add the occasional hook.

There was just one scarey moment, in the fifth, when he landed with a looping right to the body. I disguised the fact that it had hurt me and replied with a left hook counter that made Urtain more respectful, and he didn't land another really telling punch.

I gave him a real shellacking in the eighth and he was peering at me out of a badly swollen eye. A volley of punches opened a cut and the referee wisely put Urtain out of his misery by stopping the fight at the end of the round. It was curtains for Urtain.

The Aftermath

The European championship was back in Urtain's keeping the following year. I lost the title to Joe Bugner who in turn lost it to Jack Bodell. Urtain demolished Bodell in two rounds when he defended the crown for the first time in Madrid on 17 December 1971. The Basque Basher was then dethroned by German champion Jurgen Blin who lost it four months later to Joe Bugner. Talk about musical chairs!

You had to admire Urtain's staying power. He was back challenging for the title in 1977 after Bugner had been stripped of the championship by the bossy EBU who had given me the same treatment 13 years earlier. This time Urtain came a cropper when he was knocked out in four rounds by Belgian Jean-Pierre Coopman. It was the only knock-out defeat of his career.

Urtain was a classic example of a manufactured champion who had been fed a procession of pushovers and had not been able to learn his trade properly. He had all the equipment to have become a top-quality champion but had never been taught the fundamentals of the sport. If somebody had got hold of him early in his career and showed him how to jab and move he just might have become a major force in world boxing, although to be fair to him he didn't do badly for himself in his own European back yard. But he never had the necessary skill to go with his strength to trouble the top-dog Americans.

For the Record

Jose Manuel Ibar Urtain

Ht.: 5 ft. 10½ in. Wt.; 14 st.
Born San Sebastian, Spain, 14 May 1943.
Turned professional 1968.

Honours: European champion 1970, 1971–72.
Record: 66 fights, 53 wins, 3 draws, 10 losses (1 KO); 42 inside-the-distance wins (30 KOs).

14

The Fight: Joe Frazier v. Muhammad Ali
The Date: 8 March 1971
The Venue: Madison Square Garden, New
York

The Build-up

For once the fight publicists didn't have to bang their drums
and make exaggerated claims about the contestants to attract
an audience. Joe Frazier v. Muhammad Ali was a 'natural'.
It was the Irresistible Force against the Immovable Object –
and something had to give. For the first time in ring history
two undefeated heavyweights had been matched for the world
title.

It was a contest that ushered in a new era in financial as
well as fighting terms. This wasn't an old-fashioned million
dollar fight. This was the Billion Dollar Bonanza and both
Frazier and Ali were picking up an unprecedented purse of
two-and-a-half million dollars each.

I have never known a fight grab world attention to the
extent that this one did. The only ones that could have come
close to it were I suppose Tunney v. Dempsey and Louis v.
Schmeling the second time around, but that was all in the
pre-TV and satellite days. It was truly a global battle with

an estimated 300,000,000 people watching on world-wide television and at closed-circuit theatres. They didn't bother to give it the tired old tag of 'Fight of the Century'. It was simply billed as 'The Fight.' And it lived up to and beyond all expectations.

Joe Frazier had become champion in Muhammad Ali's enforced absence following his out-of-the-ring fight with the US army over his religious objections to the war in Vietnam. At 27, Frazier was two years younger than Ali, and since turning professional in 1965 had won every one of his 26 fights − all but three of them inside the distance. His idol when he was a kid, although he never saw him box, was Joe Louis. But his style was a throwback to another great world champion, Rocky Marciano.

He fought like a black Marciano with a perpetual motion two-fisted style that had earned him the nickname 'Smokin' Joe'. His physique was also similar to Rocky's. He was short by modern standards at 5 ft. 11½ in. and his reach was nine inches shorter than Ali's telescopic 82 inches. His legs were strong, his shoulders wide and − like The Rock − he was boiling with mischief and menace in the ring.

Like so many great fighters before him, Frazier had used the boxing ring to escape the poverty trap. Born at Beaufort, South Carolina, on 12 January 1944, he was the seventh son in a family of 13 and in his early days was known as Billy-Joe. His father was a farmer who scraped a living from a vegetable plantation on which Joe worked from the age of seven. He listened to tales of how Joe Louis had made a similar start in life before becoming the world's best-loved boxing champion and by the time he was nine he had made up his mind that he would become another Louis. Frazier filled old turnip sacks with moss and hung them from trees as makeshift punchbags. I guess his has been what you might call a bags-to-riches story.

Frazier followed his elder brothers to Philadelphia where he got himself a job in what was perhaps fittingly a slaughterhouse. Married at 16, Joe took up boxing seriously to keep his weight in check. He was spotted sparring at the Philadelphia Police Athletic Club by a wise old boxing trainer called Yancey 'Yank' Durham who realized his potential and helped him to get some style and technique to go with his raw power.

He won 38 of his 40 amateur contests, his two defeats both being at the massive hands of Grand Rapids giant Buster Mathis, the second set-back coming in the 1964 US Olympic trials. But the victory cost unlucky Buster a broken thumb and it was Frazier who took his place in the US team in the Tokyo Games.

Frazier won the Olympic gold medal in impressive style, soundly beating West German Hans Huber in the final. But now it was his turn to suffer from injury and when he returned to the United States he had to undergo surgery on his left hand which was placed in a plaster cast. The Olympic hero was out of work, could not box and had a wife and three kids to feed. When his plight was given publicity in the Philadelphian press the public rallied round and sent him food parcels and donations to keep him going. He finally turned professional in the summer of 1965 with a syndicate of millionaire businessmen backing him and with his old mentor Yank Durham as his manager; later ring-wise Eddie Futch joined him as his trainer.

Over the next 28 months Frazier hurried through 19 straight victories, all but two of his opponents knocked out of his path without hearing the final bell. Only Oscar Bonavena gave him real trouble and Frazier had to haul himself off the canvas twice before outpointing the durable Argentinian over ten bruising rounds.

Then, on 4 March 1968, he was matched with his old rival and bogeyman Buster Mathis in a fight billed by the New York Boxing Commission as being for the world title that had been taken away from Muhammad Ali. Frazier gave Mathis quite a mauling before forcing the referee to stop the one-way traffic in round 11.

Frazier successfully defended his title against Manuel Ramos (stopped second round), Bonavena (a clear fifteen-round points victory), Dave Zyglewicz (first-round knockout) and Jerry Quarry (stopped seventh) before being paired with WBA-recognized champion Jimmy Ellis for the undisputed title.

Ellis, Muhammad Ali's former chief sparring partner, was hammered to a fourth-round defeat, and then Frazier knocked out world light-heavyweight champion Bob Foster in two rounds to set up 'The Fight' with Ali.

The Fight

Frazier and Ali gave every indication in and out of the ring of disliking each other, but much of the hatred was manufactured for box-office business. They only really meant it inside the ring.

Ali's tongue was working overtime, not only getting publicity for the fight but also – he hoped – giving him a pyschological advantage over Frazier. But you couldn't have frightened Smokin' Joe with a gun, let alone a tongue. He was bouncing with confidence, and relaxed in between fierce training sessions by rehearsing as lead singer with his group, the Knockouts.

Everybody took it for real when the champ and challenger almost came to blows in a television studio but, being a cynical old pro and used to Ali's antics, I reckoned it was all part of the pre-fight ballyhoo.

By the time of the weigh-in, Ali and Frazier were through with insulting each other. They weighed-in separately, Frazier scaling 14 st. 9½ lb. and Ali a suprisingly heavy 15 st. 5 lb. which was the most he had weighed. Frazier predicted that he would win inside ten rounds. Ali was saying he would put out Smokin' Joe in six rounds. Nobody was betting that it would go the distance. Last word to Ali: 'If I lose I'll crawl across the ring and say, "You're the real champ of the world." '

It was like a Who's Who of boxing at the ringside. Former champions introduced from the ring included Rocky Graziano, Sugar Ray Robinson, Billy Conn, Dick Tiger, Emile Griffith, Joey Giardello, Jack Sharkey, Archie Moore, Gene Tunney and, finally, getting the loudest cheers, the old Brown Bomber Joe Louis.

Ali entered the ring wearing a blood-red dressing gown with a silver trim on it. His shorts were the same colour. Frazier wore incredible green and gold knee-length shorts that covered his tree-trunk thighs.

Ali went walkabout while they were waiting for the preliminaries, first of all slapping the champion on the shoulder and then deliberately bumping into him. While referee Arthur Mercante was giving the final instructions both Ali and Frazier were exchanging what Joe later described as 'just a little ghetto talk'. The atmosphere was so hot you could have warmed your hands on it.

I know it's easy to make judgements in hindsight but I feel that Ali took the fight six months too early. He could have done with at least one more warm-up contest following his ring-rusting lay-off. His old jab-and-dance tactics worked well in the first third of an enthralling battle as he picked off the always advancing champion with stabbing lefts and occasional left-right combinations. But Frazier just walked through the punches as if they were no more troublesome than gnat bites and concentrated his attack to the body. One left below the heart in the fourth round was so fierce that it made spectators wince.

It was from about the fifth round on that I began to form my theory that Ali had taken the fight too soon. He started to lay about on the ropes, conserving stamina but handing the initiative to the champion who kept up a non-stop bombardment of punches. It was like seeing Fred Astaire dancing down the stairs and stopping to take a breather. Ali was protecting himself well on the ropes and nullifying a lot of Frazier's work by weaving, blocking and some blatant holding. But he wasn't scoring any points himself.

They were exchanging as many words as punches and in the fifth Frazier showed that he was feeling confident by holding out his chin in taunting fashion and challenging Ali to hit him, as much as to say, 'You can't hurt me.'

The eighth was the one messy round of the fight. Ali spent so much time on the ropes that he gave the impression he was just about all in, but then, typical of the man, he confounded everybody in the ninth. Frazier appeared to have shaken him with his favourite punch, the left hook. But as he came forward to press home his advantage Ali unleashed his best attack of the fight. He poured a volley of jabs, hooks, crosses and uppercuts through Frazier's defence and the champion looked in real trouble when the bell rang.

There was a sensational moment in the tenth round when Frazier suddenly turned his back on the challenger and for a brief second looked as if he was going to quit. Arthur Mercante, an excellent referee, later revealed that in breaking up one of the numerous clinches he had accidentally caught Frazier in the eye with his outstretched fingers and it shocked the champion. But he was soon back into his all-action, walk-forward style of fighting, and continued to drive Ali back to the ropes.

The near-exhausted challenger started to wilt in the last third of the fight and had a terrible time in the thirteenth round as Frazier punished him to the head and body with a sequence of wicked hooks. Some of the punches landed in the kidney region, others to the liver and in what must have been moments of hell Ali showed to the world that he had tremendous courage and character to go with his great talent. Furthermore, he was still landing telling punches of his own, and the evidence was there for all to see in a plum-size lump that had come up on the champion's temple.

For his aggression alone Frazier had to be in front going

into the final round, and to end all arguments he climbed above his own weariness to drop Ali with the same sort of left hook with which I had floored him at Wembley Stadium more than seven years earlier. Ali crashed down on his back, his feet flying in the air. I thought I was seeing things when a shower of water seemed to splash towards him. His excitable cornerman Bundini Brown was later reported to have been fined for throwing a bucket of water over Ali while he was on the canvas! He had to summon all his strength and willpower to get himself into a standing position before the fatal ten seconds were up. Frazier roared in for the kill and clubbed Ali with a left and right to the jaw. The challenger was out on his feet but had just enough sense to know he had to back away. As he reeled towards the ropes Frazier thrashed the air with another left hook that would have certainly ended the fight if it had hit its intended target.

The full effect of the punch that had dropped Ali became apparent when the right side of his jaw began to come up like a balloon. He bravely continued to stick out the left jab that some onlookers considered had landed enough times during the furious fight to have given him the edge. But the referee and both judges called it for Frazier who was a worthy winner, while Ali – glorious in defeat – had won more fans than in any of his victories.

Frazier grabbed Ali moments after the decision had been announced and told him: 'You fought one helluva fight. You don't have to do no crawling.'

The Aftermath

The first words Ali said through his swollen jaw on his return to the dressing-room was: 'Get the guns ready. We're gonna set traps.' This was his way of saying that he was by no means finished with Frazier, who doubted whether Ali would want a return.

As it happened they had two more fights, both of them brutal affairs but nowhere near as exciting and captivating as *the fight* in New York. Ali outpointed Frazier over twelve rounds for the US heavyweight championship on 28 January 1974, and then forced him to retire at the end of 13 viciously punishing rounds in their 'Thriller in Manila' world title battle on 1 October 1975.

Ali and Frazier gave each other such a hiding in their first fight that both finished up in hospital. Ali had to have treatment to his jaw and Frazier was reportedly flat on his back for two weeks recovering from the after-effects of a war that later contests were to prove took more out of the winner than the loser.

Frazier purposely took things easy for the next 20 months. He successfully defended the championship against two hand-picked challengers, Terry Daniels (stopped four rounds) and Ron Stander (stopped four rounds). But you can't keep getting away with easy pickings when you are the world champion and the Frazier camp had to accept a genuine challenger in the formidable figure of George Foreman. I'll come to that fight later, but first I'll give you my version of the final fling of my career against one Joe Bugner.

For the Record

Joe Frazier

Born Beaufort, South Carolina, 12 January 1944.
Ht.: 5 ft. 11½ in. Wt.: 14 st. 6 lb.
1964 Olympic heavyweight champion.
Turned professional 1965. Managed by Yank Durham.
Honours: world heavyweight champion 1968–73.
Record: 36 fights, 32 wins, 4 losses (no KOs); 27 inside-the-
    distance wins (10 KOs).

15
The Fight: Joe Bugner v. Henry Cooper
The Date: 16 March 1971
The Venue: Wembley Arena

The Build-up

I didn't make it public but I had decided to hang up my gloves after defending my British, European and Commonwealth titles against Joe Bugner; and I was determined to go out as a winner.

Not counting the brief period when I gave up my championship in protest over the lack of support from the British Boxing Board of Control, I had held the title for a span of twelve years and was proud of the fact that I had taken on and beaten all comers. Joe Erskine, Brian London, Dick Richardson, Johnny Prescott, Jack Bodell and Billy Walker had each been given their chance to take the crown and I had beaten them all. There was no way I was going to let a relative novice like Bugner ruin my record.

Bugner was just three days past his 21st birthday, while I was a couple of months short of my 37th. I reckoned I had forgotten more than he had learned about the game and I was confident I could mess him about and cancel out the age difference by intelligent pacing and careful conservation of energy.

Despite being knocked out in his professional debut, Bugner had proved he had got a strong chin and I trained with a distance fight in mind. He had a superbly sculptured physique, standing 6 ft. 4 in. and weighing near to 16 st. at his peak. In his schooldays he was one of Britain's finest young discus throwers and he was built just like one of those statues of a Greek discus-throwing hero. But, to be brutally honest, I thought he often used to look like a statue in the ring. Joe was not a natural, instinctive fighter. His manager, a livewire Anglo-Scot called Andy Smith, had done a marvellous job moulding and manufacturing him into an orthodox but predictable stand-up boxer. He had spotted this young boy blessed with an impressive physique and set about trying to shape him into a world beater. It was a real Svengali job and Smith was aided and abetted by some shrewd matchmaking by Mickey Duff.

Bugner's life story was like something out of *Boy's Own*. He was born in Hungary and was just six at the time of the 1956 Hungarian revolution that triggered an invasion by Russian troops. Joe's family joined the flood of refugees escaping from Hungary and they got aboard a ship which they thought was taking them to the United States. But they wound up in Britain, first of all in a refugee camp and then in a family home in Bedfordshire where Joe revealed his sporting prowess. He was an outstanding schoolboy athlete, though it was not until he was 15 that he showed any interest in boxing. Just two years later he was making his professional debut under Andy Smith's guidance.

Young Joe was knocked out in the third round of his first contest against unsung Paul Brown, a defeat he avenged six months later. His 15th opponent, Ulrich Regis, sadly collapsed and died after a points defeat and this tragedy weighed heavily on Bugner who was by then 18 and carrying the responsibility of being a husband and a father.

By the time he got round to challenging me for the titles Bugner had fought 31 times, winning 29 and drawing one. He had fought only four or five opponents of any real quality and in the case of both Johnny Prescott (won points, eight rounds) and Brian London (referee stopped in the fifth) both were having the final fights of their careers and were way past the peak of their powers and of their ambition.

Bugner had not won the public over to his side because too many of his performances were quite pedestrian and unexciting. He so much *looked* the part with his giant build that fans expected fireworks from him but too often all they got was a damp squib. I had been able to take a good look at him on his rise up the ladder and was as confident as I had ever been that I could win when I stepped into the Wembley ring for the last fight of my career.

The Fight

You can't beat an old champion against a young prospect for setting boxing arenas alight and there was a tremendous atmosphere at Wembley. Most of the 'experts' had gone for a Bugner victory because they considered that a combination of my suspect eyes and old legs would let me down against a strong, young opponent who had a reach, height and weight advantage.

But I had trained as conscientiously for this fight as if it were for the world title and I knew I was fit enough to go the full 15 rounds if necessary. The referee for the contest was Harry Gibbs, a docks worker who was generally considered the best third man in the business.

My fight plan was to try to keep Bugner on his back foot because he was not nearly as forceful when he was having to box on the retreat. His strongest weapon was a long, solid left lead and I knew I had to block it or make him miss and then counter with my own jabs. I deliberately started at a

slow pace because I wanted to have something in reserve for the later rounds when I planned to put my foot on the accelerator.

It was a battle of the jabs and for ten rounds neither Bugner nor I could have claimed that we were in command. At the end of the tenth, my manager Jim Wicks leant through the ropes and talked into my ear. 'Now we've got to step up the pace,' he said. 'We've let this geezer get on top too much.'

I reckon the fight was even-stevens at the two-thirds mark. In rounds 11, 12, 13 and 14 I took the fight to Bugner, beating him to the jab and doubling up my punches to the head and increasing my output at the inside exchanges. There was no doubt in my mind that I had won those four rounds and so, as I went out for the fifteenth, and the final round of my career, I felt in my heart that Bugner had to knock me out to win.

Joe had obviously been told that he was trailing because he dug down into his boots and produced a grandstand finish. I met him halfway but, being charitable, I'll concede that he won the round. But I was positive that I had won the fight and I walked towards Harry Gibbs with my hand outstretched for him to go through the formality of raising my arm as the victor and still British, European and Commonwealth champion.

You could have knocked me down with a featherweight when Gibbs brushed past me and went to Bugner's corner and – to Joe's utter disbelief – raised his hand. I have never been so shocked, stunned, speechless – you name it – in my life. All I could find to say was, 'Cor stone me.' Or bleep-bleep words to that effect. My brother George had his arms wrapped round Jim Wicks who was in the mood to give Harry Gibbs a right-hander. In a long and distinguished refereeing career, Gibbs has quite rightly gained the respect of the boxing world. But on this night he had dropped a right clanger. Wembley rocked with the boos of the crowd who agreed with my assessment of the fight. Nearly every ringside reporter had me winning it and from the astonished looks on the faces of Bugner's cornermen they also thought I'd retained my titles.

The Aftermath

I've often heard it said that my going out on a sea of sympathy because I'd been robbed added to my popularity with the public. Maybe that's so, but I'd much rather have won their respect by going out as a winner and undefeated champion. Anyway, it's all history now and I hope you don't think I've been whingeing too much in this chapter. It's just that even more than 14 years later I still get the ache when I remember how Harry Gibbs walked right past me and held up Bugner's hand. That night I was the victim of a robbery with violence.

Any old how, the king was dead. Long live the king. But just six months later Joe went and lost the titles to Jack Bodell in a mauling contest that was not exactly one of the most enthralling championship fights of all time. He just didn't seem to have his heart in the fight that night and won only one of the 15 rounds against an opponent I had well beaten in two title fights.

Bugner was nothing if not brilliantly manoeuvred and within little more than a year he had leap-frogged into a European championship fight with Jurgen Blin, knocking the German out in the eighth round with one of the best right-hand punches he ever threw.

In 1973 he became the only man to fight Muhammad Ali and Joe Frazier in back-to-back contests. He was beaten each time on points over 12 rounds in non-title matches but gave a good account of himself in both fights. On 1 July 1975 he had a re-match with Ali in Kuala Lumpur and this time the world championship was at stake. Both Ali and Bugner were drained by the sweltering-hot conditions and it was one of the dullest and least memorable of all Ali's title fights. Joe just fought to survive and was well beaten on points in a tedious fight that was often more like 'Come Dancing' than a world heavyweight championship contest.

Bugner relinquished his European championship to concentrate on trying to get back into contention for the world title against ranked opponents, rather than having the EBU pick his fights. Then, out of the blue, he suddenly announced his retirement in January 1976, at the age of 25.

I thought at the time it was some sort of gimmick and, sure enough, there was Joe announcing his comeback just six months later.

While he was out of action, Yorkshire southpaw Richard Dunn had taken over as British, European and Commonwealth champion. He was a good banger but had a suspect chin. Joe found the point of his jaw with a couple of fierce right crosses and Dunn was 'done' in the first round without landing a blow in anger. It was welcome aggression from Bugner and I wondered how much more successful he might have been had he showed this attitude earlier in his career.

Bugner's domestic life got into something of a distasteful tangle and he went off to live in the United States and popped up as a hammy-looking actor in a couple of spaghetti westerns. Then he made another comeback under the unlikely guidance of his second wife, Marlene, a tough Australian journalist.

He started to try to be a fighter rather than a jab-and-move boxer and came unstuck against the only class men that he met – Earnie Shavers and Marvis Frazier. Joe was new promoter Frank Warren's trump card in his bid to make an impact on the London boxing scene and ITV featured a series of fights in which, to be honest, Bugner didn't cover himself with glory against some mediocre opponents.

To me, Joe Bugner was like a volcano that never erupted. There was always more promise and potential than actual achievement. Despite all my moaning about the way he was given a verdict over me, I have never held anything against him personally. He was a likeable giant but lacked that certain charisma that cements fighters into the hearts of the fans.

For the Record

Joe Bugner

Born Hungary, 13 March 1950.
Ht.: 6 ft. 4 in. Wt.: 16 st.
Turned professional at the age of 17. Managed by Andy Smith.
Honours: British, European and Commonwealth champion.
Record: 70 fights, 58 wins, 1 draw, 11 losses (1 KO); 39 inside-
the-distance wins (6 KOs).

16

The Fight: George Foreman v. Joe Frazier
The Date: 22 January 1973
The Venue: Kingston, Jamaica

The Build-up

George Foreman was the sort of fighter my old manager Jim Wicks used to call 'too ugly'. It wasn't said in derogatory terms but was meant as an indication to promoters that we wouldn't touch him with a barge pole, let alone a left jab. Sonny Liston and Joe Frazier came into the same category.

Jim never believed in pushing me into a fight just for the sake of the money. If he thought an opponent was too dangerous or had a style that would give me problems, he would simply say to Jack Solomons, Harry Levene or whoever was trying to make the match: 'We ain't interested, thank you. He's too ugly.' There was a year or two when Foreman looked just about the 'ugliest' fighter of all time. He had all the physical attributes to stand eyeball to eyeball with the biggest opponents in what had become a *super* heavyweight division. He was just a fraction off 6 ft. 4 in. tall, weighed close to 16 st. and had a 78½ in. reach that enabled him do damaging work from a distance.

Like so many championship contenders, Foreman had come up the hard way. He was born in a black ghetto at Marshall, Texas, on 10 January 1948, the fifth of seven children of a railroad construction labourer.

Many of his early years were spent on the wrong side of the tracks and on the wrong side of the law, and after dropping out of high school at 14 he wasted most of his time hanging round with street gangs in a notoriously tough area of Houston known as the Bloody Fifth Ward.

Boxing rescued him from sliding into a life of crime. He was persuaded to join America's Jobs Corps and was sent to a special work centre at Pleasonton, California, where he not only learnt bricklaying and carpentry but also how to use his fists in a legal manner. It was December 1966 when Foreman, aged 18, pulled on a pair of boxing gloves for the first time. There was a gymnasium at the centre and Foreman's potential was spotted by the resident trainer Nick 'Doc' Broadus. He encouraged George to take boxing seriously and taught him the basics of a solid left jab and how to construct a sound defence.

The rest Broadus knew he could leave to nature because Foreman had enormous natural strength. George learnt his lessons well and within two years had emerged as America's outstanding amateur heavyweight boxer and he represented the United States in the 1968 Olympics in Mexico. These were the games in which track athletes Tommie Smith and John Carlos caused uproar by using the medal ceremony as a platform for a 'black power' demonstration.

When Foreman duly won the gold medal by pounding Russian Ionas Chepulis to a two-round defeat – and so succeeding Joe Frazier as champion – everybody in the United States held their breath when he climbed onto the victory rostrum. They wondered whether he would turn the ceremony into a political statement.

It so happened that George wasn't into the 'black power' stuff and thousands of Americans rose and applauded their television sets when he took a small Stars and Stripes flag out of his dressing-gown pocket and waved it while standing with the gold medal round his neck. It was a patriotic gesture that won him millions of fans. Foreman was ready to show the world 'black power' of a more basic kind.

He had a queue of managers and business syndicates chasing him for his signature and he finally elected to turn professional under the guidance of Dick Sadler, an old-time vaudeville song-and-dance man who was steeped in boxing and had worked as a trainer with Archie Moore and Sonny Liston.

Foreman began his professional career on 23 June 1969, with a third-round stoppage of Don Waldheim on a Madison Square Garden bill topped by Joe Frazier against Jerry Quarry. He had started the way he intended to continue. In his first 38 paid fights – all won – only three men managed to stay the course, and of the 35 opponents he stopped or knocked out only three survived more than four rounds. In 1972 he had five contests and won each of them by a clean knock-out, each time in the second round.

World champion Smokin' Joe Frazier was biding his time waiting for a record cash haul for a second title defence against Muhammad Ali. It was decided he could do with a 'warm up' fight while waiting for the Ali return. His handlers studied Foreman's record and arrived at the conclusion that he had been fed on a diet of pushover opponents. On paper, there was certainly some justification for this verdict because, to be honest, I had heard of only a couple of the guys Foreman had been knocking over. Yet there was a certain savagery about the way he had disposed of the opposition, however weak, that should have sounded a danger warning in the complacent Frazier camp. They went ahead and negotiated a voluntary defence. It proved one of the most costly blunders in world heavyweight championship history.

The Fight

Foreman was a 3–1 underdog when he climbed into the ring in the National Stadium in Kingston, Jamaica. The concensus of opinion was that 29-year-old Frazier would be able to take his best shots and then wear the 25-year-old challenger down with his usual aggressive, all-action style. Most fight experts chose to ignore the fact that Foreman had advantages in height (four inches), weight (four pounds) and reach (five inches).

At the first bell Frazier came bouncing forward as he had in all his previous fights. Instead of retreating Foreman stood his ground and there was something akin to an explosion in the centre of the ring. The challenger had built a reputation as being a mighty banger with his right hand but it was quickly evident that he could also whack with his left. As Frazier attempted to bull his way forward Foreman hit him with a stream of long lefts and rights as casually as if he was in a gymnasium workout. The champion tried to reply with a two-fisted attack but he was wildly off with his timing and distance.

Suddenly Foreman took deliberate aim with a long, clubbing right that thumped against Frazier's jaw and sent him backwards onto the seat of his pants. It would be wrong to say that the champion didn't know what had hit him because he did. He saw it coming but it homed in on its target like a guided missile and he just couldn't get out of the way.

Frazier rose unsteadily at two and stood staring at Foreman in something close to disbelief as referee Arthur Mercante called the mandatory eight seconds. In those few moments the champion convinced himself that it was just a fluke punch and decided to put the challenger in his place. He went charging at Foreman and landed his favourite punch, the left hook to the jaw. I think it hurt Joe almost as much as the blows from Foreman when the challenger shrugged off the punch as if it was no more troublesome than a weak slap.

From that moment on it was all Foreman. He drove Frazier back to the ropes with a series of jabs and then five successive rights to the head dropped the champion like a sack of potatoes. He jumped up immediately but it was already obvious that he was completely outgunned. It was also clear that he was nothing like as powerful a machine as he had been before his painfully earned victory over Muhammad Ali. As the bell rang to end the sensational first round Frazier was back on the canvas with the count at two. The champion decided that if he was going to go down it would be with all guns blazing.

He came running out of his corner at the start of the second round but managed only to rush straight into a jolting left and a following right to the chin. This time he stayed down for the mandatory eight count. Poor old Joe was now fighting in a daze. He was a standing target for Foreman's heavy long-range punches and after a left-right-left-right combination to the head he collapsed backwards for a fifth count.

Frazier was bravely up at eight but was now a pathetic puppet of a figure who had lost control of his legs. He stumbled forward and was literally lifted off his feet by a right uppercut and he crashed down on to his knees. As he knelt trying to listen to the count his head lolled on one side and he was trying to push his blood-stained gumshield back into his mouth but couldn't quite get his co-ordination right.

It was now frightening to watch and even Foreman was pleading with Frazier to stay down. 'Stay there, Joe,' he shouted. 'You've taken enough.' Somehow Frazier pulled himself up for a sixth time but, thank goodness, the referee moved forward to stop the annihilation after just one minute 35 seconds of the second round.

It was Foreman's sixth successive second-round knock-out victory. Frazier had kissed goodbye not only to his championship but also to a multi-million dollar match with Ali.

The Aftermath

Once he had recovered his senses Frazier stated the obvious at the after-fight inquest. 'We underrated him,' he said. 'We were fooled into thinking it would be easy. Foreman was just too strong for me. He caught me early and I was never able to recover and get my act together. I've blown the fight with Ali but I'll get round to him after I've had a return with Foreman.'

But it was two and a half years before Frazier got his chance to try to avenge that terrible defeat in Jamaica. By then he had lost two punishing fights against Ali, and Foreman was an ex-champion with little appetite left for the game. Joe went to extraordinary lengths to try to get a pyschological advantage over Foreman. He climbed into the ring at Uniondale on 15 June 1976 with a dressing-gown hood covering his head. When he removed the hood just moments before the first bell it was revealed that he had shaved all the hair off his head. It certainly made him *look* more menacing but Foreman was totally unimpressed and gave him another tanking before the referee rescued Frazier in the fifth round.

This was Joe's last stand. He kept threatening to come out of retirement but left the real action to his heavyweight son Marvis who was rushed too quickly into a fight with Larry Holmes and was blasted to a first-round defeat.

Frazier, at his peak, was one of the great champions but his style of fighting left him too exposed to punches and in George Foreman he found an opponent who was simply too big and strong for him. Or, as my dear old manager Jim Wicks would have said, he was 'too ugly' for him.

For the Record

George Foreman

Born Marshall, Texas, 10 January 1948.

My Most Memorable Fights

Ht.: 6 ft. 3½ in. Wt.: 15 st. 12 lb.
Olympic heavyweight champion 1968.
Turned professional 1969. Managed by Dick Sadler.
Record: 47 fights, 45 wins, 2 losses (1 KO); 42 inside-the-distance
    wins (27 KOs).

17
The Fight: Muhammad Ali v. George
Foreman
The Date: 30 October 1974
The Venue: Kinshasa, Zaire

The Build-up

This was known as the 'Rumble in the Jungle'. There has
never been a world heavyweight championship fight quite
like it and I doubt if there will ever be one like it again. It was
sponsored by the government of Zaire, with their President
Mobutu taking a personal interest in the promotion. President
Mobutu saw the staging of the fight as a great propaganda
platform for his country. Zaire suddenly became known to
millions of people around the world who could not have told
you where on earth it was before George Foreman agreed to
put his title on the line in a stadium built in what was a
jungle clearing on the outskirts of Zaire's capital of Kinshasa.

With the greatest respect to Foreman, it has to be said that
it was the phenomenal popularity of Ali that was the main
attraction. The Zaire government were prepared to invest $12
million in the promotion only if Ali was the challenger.

It was a bright, young London businessman, John Daly,
who had laid the foundation for this extraordinary promotion

when the company he ran with film star David Hemmings – Hemdale Leisure Corporation – put up the original million and a half dollars with which American promoter Don King started the ball rolling.

It was a tremendously proud moment for John's father George Daly, a former highly skilled professional boxer whose career spanned the Second World War. George had boxed out of Blackfriars and I wondered just what he must have thought of his son from South London helping to organize a world heavyweight championship fight in deepest Africa.

Foreman was a warm favourite to keep the title he had taken from Joe Frazier in such devastating fashion in Jamaica 21 months earlier. Since becoming champion he had successfully defended the championship twice. He had knocked out little-known Joe Roman in one round in Tokyo on 1 September 1973, and had then taken on Ken Norton, the top-quality Californian heavyweight who had won and lost in two battles with Ali.

Many good fight judges thought Norton would give Foreman a lot of trouble when they met for the title down in Caracas, Venezuela, on 26 March 1974, but the champion bombed him out in two rounds. It meant that Foreman's last eight fights had occupied just 15 rounds! There was no doubt that the man carried dynamite in his fists and the general view was that Ali, at 32, would not be able to stand up to the sort of hammering that Foreman could hand out.

Since his failure to regain the world title from Joe Frazier in 1971 Ali had lost one of 14 fights, a points defeat by Ken Norton during which he had suffered a broken jaw. Ali gained revenge in the return fight, and on 28 January wiped out the only other blot on his record when he outpointed Frazier over 12 rounds in New York to set up the 'Rumble in the Jungle' with Foreman.

The Fight

Foreman was cut over an eye during a sparring session in Zaire just eight days before the fight and the contest had to be put back for a month. There is nothing more frustrating for a boxer than to have a fight date postponed. You get yourself mentally and physically tuned for a certain time and a certain place and it can throw you completely when there is a late change of plans.

Ali cleverly used the delay to his advantage by stepping up his training sessions with a string of sparring partners including a young unbeaten fighter called Larry Holmes. He became completely acclimatized to the humid atmosphere in equatorial Zaire and gathered a growing fan club of Africans who clearly idolized him.

It sounded almost as if Ali was boxing at home when he left his dressing-room for the long walk to the ring for the 4 a.m. punch-up. The fight had been timed to attract peak-time viewing audiences around the world and it was estimated that more than 300 million people were glued to television and closed-circuit screens. Foreman and Ali were being paid five million dollars each. For that sort of money they didn't care what the hands on the clock said.

There was a mightly roar from the crowd when Ali climbed through the ropes and walked majestically around waving to the spectators from all corners of the ring as if he were the champion. Foreman's greeting was mooted by comparison. There was no question about whose side the African fans were on.

Before the fight, Ali had been told over and over again not to get trapped on the ropes where Foreman was considered to be at his most dangerous. So everybody, Foreman included, expected Ali to be up on his toes and dancing. Typically of Ali he did the exact opposite to what we all anticipated. After a first round in which he jabbed and moved in his familiar style he took every opportunity to back on to the ropes and almost encouraged the champion to throw punches at him. Foreman duly obliged and must have hammered in more than a hundred blows during the course of the fight. A lot of them got through to Ali's body but he also blocked many of the punches on his elbows and gloves.

All the time that he was laying back on the ropes conserving energy in the stamina-sapping conditions Ali kept talking to the champion. 'I thought you could punch. . . . Is that the best you can do, sissy? . . . You're just a chump, not a champ . . . Where's your punch, sucker? You ain't got nuthin'!'

Referee Zack Clayton kept warning Ali that he would disqualify him if he didn't cut out the talking but crafty old Muhammad knew there was no way he would dare throw him out of the ring because it would have caused a riot. He kept up the talking to gain a pyschological advantage over Foreman, conning him into thinking that his punches were not hurting.

It was something close to self-hynopsis by Ali because there was no doubt that the champion was landing with the sort of heavy ammunition that had flattened a procession of fighters. But the challenger was shrugging them off and inviting Foreman to try again.

God knows what damage those punches were doing to Ali, but I'm sure a lot of them must have caught up with him after his retirement from the ring. No man on earth could have shifted those sort of powerhouse blows without them having some effect. But that moonlit night in Zaire Ali convinced the champion and the crowd that he was some sort of superhuman. He took the best punches that Foreman could throw and still he kept on talking as if he could not feel them. At the end of every round Ali conducted his army of fans in a rehearsed chant, 'Ali! Ali! Bomaye! Ali! Ali! Bomaye.' Roughly translated, 'bomaye' means 'knock him dead'. By the seventh round it was becoming clear that Foreman was knocking himself dead. He had just about punched himself out and was so tired he could hardly lift his arms. It was not just physical tiredness. Ali had 'psyched' all the fight out of him. Foreman was a fighter used to seeing opponents fall over when he hit them, yet here was Ali taking his best shots and then telling him over and over again: 'You're a chump, not a champ.'

At the end of every round Ali had come off the ropes firing lefts and rights. It was almost as if he was holding a rehearsal for what was to be the finish of the fight. Foreman had virtually to drag himself out for the eighth round, lumbering to the centre of the ring in what looked an impersonation of the 'Mummy' that Ali had nicknamed him before the fight. Ali lured him towards the ropes as if he was about to rest back on them again, using what he later described as his 'rope-a-dope' tactics. But this time he catapulted forward and crashed a beauty of a straight right to the point of Foreman's jaw.

The champion half turned and folded to the canvas almost in slow motion. He was already suffering from exhaustion and the punch had now scattered his senses. At the count of ten he was on his feet but in no position to defend himself and the referee signalled the first knock-out defeat of his career.

The crowd went berserk. Ali had become only the second heavyweight champion to regain the title. 'Ali! Ali! Bomaye! Ali! Ali! Bomaye!' they chanted. Foreman had been knocked dead. The one and only Ali was back on the throne where he belonged.

The Aftermath

George Foreman was never the same fighter or even the same man after his defeat in Zaire. Ali knocked not only the confidence but also the heart out of him. Foreman had come late to boxing and had experienced only the glory of winning. Only people really in love with the game stay totally committed when they realize just how bitter can be the taste of defeat.

It transpired after the Ali fight that all had not been well in the Foreman camp. It was suggested that Foreman had been given the wrong fight instructions by manager Dick Sadler and ex-world champion advisers Archie Moore and Sandy Saddler. Foreman also complained that his hotel accommodation had been too noisy, hinted that his food and drink had been tampered with, said the ring ropes were too loose and that the referee had given him a quick count. They were pretty pathetic excuses by a fallen idol who had been as much kidded out of the championship as knocked out. Ali was simply too mentally alert for him.

Foreman got himself new direction, switching to the guidance of the respected and knowledgable Gil Clancy, but he had left his appetite for boxing behind him in Zaire. Apart from meaningless exhibitions, he was out of action for more than a year before making a comeback against Ron Lyle. He had to climb off the canvas before winning by a fifth-round knock-out and it was clear that he was no longer the formidable force of the pre-Ali days when he had looked just about invincible. He confirmed his superiority over a worn-out Joe Frazier with a victory in five rounds and then, after wins against three undistinguished opponents, was matched with Jimmy Young in what was billed as a world title eliminator to find a challenger to Muhammad Ali. Foreman gave a feeble display against Young and was taken to hospital suffering from exhaustion after being knocked down in the 12th and last round on the way to a points defeat.

It was then that we found out why Foreman had become just a shadow of the fighter who had become world champion in such devastating style four years earlier. George had got religion. He said that he had seen signs that the Lord wanted him to hang up his gloves and that he considered it sinful to try to hit and hurt another man. Foreman announced that he was giving up boxing to become an evangelist, punching the Bible instead of chins. He returned to the street corners where he had misspent his youth to try to convince young blacks that they should turn away from violence and drugs. The last I heard he had blown up to more than 20 stone and was unrecognizable from the fearsome fighter who had terrorized the heavyweight division.

George Foreman had come into boxing like a lion and had gone out like a lamb.

18

The Fight: Muhammad Ali v. Leon Spinks
The Date: 15 September 1978
The Venue: New Orleans Superdome

The Build-up

The world heavyweight championship is the greatest prize in sport and I thought Muhammad Ali was cheapening the title when he agreed to defend it against Leon Spinks, a virtual novice whose professional ring experience stretched to just seven fights. It was not even as if he had won them all. Scott LeDoux, an ordinary journeyman, had held him to a draw over ten rounds in his sixth contest, but this was not allowed to interfere with negotiations for a championship fight that, on paper, looked a farcical mismatch.

The slender thread on which the publicists sold the fight was that Spinks had won the Olympic light-heavyweight gold medal in Montreal in 1976 — 16 years after Ali (then Cassius Clay) had won the same title. What they didn't add is that Ali had then fought nineteen times and was a seasoned professional by the time he got his shot at the title.

I thought Spinks getting a championship chance was a scandal almost on a par with the one when 1956 Olympic heavyweight champion Pete Rademacher was manoeuvred into a title fight with Floyd Patterson on his professional debut. Rademacher was knocked out in six rounds. The sensational difference with Spinks is that he shook everybody – particularly Ali – by winning the fight and the title! It was one of the boxing upsets of the century.

It was a slums-to-stardom story for Spinks that even an overimaginative Hollywood scriptwriter would have hesitated to submit. Born on 11 July 1953, he was the eldest of seven children raised in a rough, tough St Louis ghetto. Spinks learnt to fight in the mean streets where muggers and drug-pushers held power. It was street fights that cost him his two front teeth, causing the gap that later became his trademark.

His parents separated when he was ten and he was brought up by his mother, who taught Bible classes at home while keeping the impoverished family going with welfare money. Leon had grown up terrified of his bullying father who once punished him by suspending him from a nail in the wall and then pummelling him as if he were a punchbag. That sort of experience breeds a special type of person and Leon grew up sullen and suspicious.

His father continually told him that he would never amount to anything. 'That was my greatest incentive,' he said years later after finding fame with his fists. 'I was determined to prove him wrong and become a somebody.'

Leon began conventional boxing at a St Louis community centre where his younger brother, Michael, was his regular sparring partner. After dropping out of high school in the tenth grade, Leon eventually joined the Marine Corps and its élite Camp Lejeune boxing squad. He unloaded all his in-built aggression in the ring and quickly became a leading amateur.

Both he and his brother Michael won places in the US team for the 1976 Olympics in Montreal, Leon at light-heavy-weight and Michael at middleweight. They were prominent members of a brilliant US squad and became the first brothers to win Olympic boxing gold medals in the same Games. Among their team-mates were Sugar Ray Leonard, Howard Davis and John Tate, all of whom became successful professionals – but none with the indecent haste of Leon Spinks.

The exposure of Leon's Olympic triumph on television meant he was suddenly 'a somebody' and the professional touts were quickly queuing up for his signature. He got an early discharge from the US Marines, moved to Philadelphia with his wife Nova and his stepdaughter, and turned pro under the supervision of big-fight promoter Bob Arum.

The emergence of Spinks as a world championship challenger had links more with John L. Baird than John L. Sullivan. He was very much a product of the television age, with six of his first seven fights being featured coast-to-coast on CBS. A lot of modern fighters owe their fortunes to John Logie Baird's invention of television.

Since his recapture of the world championship, Muhammad Ali had accounted for Chuck Wepner (stopped 15th), Ron Lyle (stopped 11th), Joe Bugner (clear points win), Joe Frazier (retired at the end of 13 wickedly punishing rounds), Jean Pierre Coopman (stopped fifth), Jimmy Young (disputed points decision), Richard Dunn (fifth-round knockout), Ken Norton (narrow points win), Alfredo Evangelista (clear points win) and Earnie Shavers (clear points win). He was looking for an easy defence while waiting for a big-money battle with Ken Norton to materialize. Leon Spinks looked just the job.

Ali totally underestimated Spinks and was far too casual in his approach to the fight. He was slow and sluggish against an enthusiastic young challenger who forced a fast pace throughout 15 rounds to earn a split points decision.

I was mightily impressed by Spinks who fought out of his skin, but I was concerned by Ali's performance. He looked nothing like the old Ali who had thrilled and entertained millions of fight fans for more than a decade with his twinkling feet, fast fists and even faster tongue. What a sad way, I thought, for a legend to end.

But I should have known better. Ali, as usual, had a sensation up his sleeve. He called it the 'Second Coming'.

The Fight

There was, inevitably, a return which was billed as the Battle of New Orleans and Ali had hinted that it could be his last stand. Could he become the first man in history to regain the world heavyweight championship a second time? At 36 the odds seemed against him. But it was the sort of situation on which Ali thrived. Nothing gave him greater motivation than being able to prove people wrong.

He got himself back into superb condition and was ready to fight with a fierce concentration that he had not shown since his third duel with Joe Frazier – the 'Thriller in Manila' that knocked the hell out of both champion and challenger.

Meantime, Spinks had found it difficult to conduct himself as heavyweight champion of the world. In the six months that he had held the title he had been surrounded by undesirable hangers-on, had had problems with the police and had lived a life in the fast lane which was no preparation for a return fight with a man as determined on winning as Ali.

From the opening seconds of the first round it was evident that only the names were the same as in their Las Vegas fight in February. Ali took command straight away by getting up on his toes and dancing in the old-fashioned way. There was no suicidal rope-a-dope tactics. He kept on the move and never had his left hand out of the champion's face.

In their first fight Spinks had swarmed all over Ali. This time Ali was not there to be hit. He floated like a butterfly and stung like a bee, just as in his peak years. It was as if Ali had not only shed weight but also several years. Every time Spinks tried to get to close quarters Ali met him with a

151

tattoo of left-right combinations to the head, then he would grab the champion with old-pro holds that exposed Leon's lack of experience. When they first met Spinks had fought the way he had wanted. This time Ali made him fight the way *he* wanted him to fight.

Ali was way ahead on all scorecards going into the last third of the fight and the only question was: how long can he keep up this pace? For Ali, the answer was 15 masterful rounds. It was Spinks who struggled to last the course and it was later revealed that he had skipped several workouts to enjoy the good life. Ali made him pay for his lack of professionalism and was a runaway points winner, thus becoming the first man in ring history to capture the world heavyweight championship three times.

That should have been enough to satisfy any man. But this was not any man. This was the one and only Muhammad Ali.

The Aftermath

A saddened but suddenly more experienced Spinks said after losing the crown he had worn for just 212 days: 'My heart wasn't in it like it should have been. I had a lot of things on my mind, problems the heavyweight championship brought me. I guess I just didn't know how to handle it. It all happened so fast.'

There were even bigger problems around the corner for Spinks. While his brother, Michael, became the rising star and eventually one of the great world light-heavyweight champions, Leon's star crashed in a mess of his own making. He was stopped in one disastrous round by South African Gerrie Coetzee in Monte Carlo on 24 June 1979, and then got himself involved with all the wrong kinds of people again. There was talk of drug scandals, confrontations with the police, and divorce proceedings that brought him more negative publicity. The American media referred to him as a 'man-child' and he just didn't have the intelligence or the maturity to handle all the pressures that ring fame heaped on him.

His boxing career inevitably suffered and he was no match for Larry Holmes when he challenged for the world title again in Detroit on 12 June 1981. Holmes flattened Spinks in three one-sided rounds to end whatever ambitions he had of ruling the world's heavyweights again.

So he set his sights on the cruiserweight championship, but, after a creditable points victory over Jesse Burnett, he came totally unstuck against Carlos De Leon in Atlantic City on 6 March 1983. Spinks took a lot of heavy hammer before the referee stopped the fight at the end of six punishing rounds.

He disappeared from the fight scene for two years – to rededicate himself to God, so the publicists informed us – and then started a comeback at the age of 31 in March 1985. Spinks, looking sluggish compared with the young whipper-snapper who had swarmed all over Muhammad Ali in their first fight, stopped unranked Mexican Lupe Guerra in four rounds. The fight was made at 13 st 13 lbs and Spinks weighed in one pound overweight after apparently shedding six pounds in the 24 hours before the contest. It was not the most professional way to make a comeback.

I wonder just what sort of career Leon might have had if he had not been rushed into world heavyweight championship contention before he was really ready for it? His victory over Ali was a freak affair and lifted him into a pressure-cooker situation in which he got himself badly burned. Sudden fame can often be as hard to handle as sudden disaster. Leon just could not cope with the awesome responsibilities of being heavyweight champion of the world.

Explaining his struggle to adjust, Leon – or was it his publicity man? – came out with the memorable line: 'You can take the man out of the ghetto, but you can't take the ghetto out of the man.'

Had he laid a proper foundation to his career he just might have become as well established in championship class as his brother Michael, who took the conventional route to his world title and once he had arrived at the top was well capable of looking after himself both inside and out of the ring. Leon had the talent. What he lacked was the dedication, experience and commitment to hang on to the greatest prize in sport.

For the Record

Leon Spinks

Born St Louis, 11 July 1953.
Ht.: 6 ft. 2 in. Wt.: 13 st. 12 lb.
Olympic light-heavyweight champion 1976.
Turned professional 1977. Managed at the start by Bob Arum.
Record: 19 fights, 13 wins, 2 draws, 4 losses (no KOs); 8 inside-the-distance wins (5 KOs).

19
The Fight: Larry Holmes v. Muhammad Ali
The Date: 2 October 1980
The Venue: Caesar's Palace, Las Vegas

The Build-up

This was supposed to be Muhammad Ali's 'Last Hurrah', a
final comeback to capture the world heavyweight championship for an unprecedented fourth time. But for once his mind
and his pride were making an appointment his body could
not keep. Waiting for him in the opposite corner was Larry
Holmes, his former sparring partner whom Ali saw as a
pretender to his throne.

Early in his career Holmes had idolized Ali to such an
extent that the first time Muhammad blackened his eye in
the gym he declined treatment until he could get a photogra-
pher. 'I wanted evidence of what the great man had done to
me,' he said.

In Ali's estimation Holmes was fighting above his station.
He still considered him in the sparring partner bracket and
could not accept that he had improved out of all recognition
from the young boxer he used to hire at 100 dollars a session;
neither could he see, as we who looked sadly on could see,

that he himself had lost much of the magic and mastery that had made him a fighting phenomenon.

Ali had been tempted out of a two-year retirement by the promise of an $8 million purse. But it was more than profit at stake. It was pride. His giant ego wouldn't allow him to concede that his one-time hired hand had taken over as the bossman. Holmes, winner of all his 35 fights, was determined to make it a case of 'the ego has landed'.

Since his defeat of Leon Spinks in 1978 Ali had ballooned to a fat, grossly overweight 18 stone. But from the moment he signed to fight Holmes in a 25,000-seat temporary arena specially built in the Caesar's Palace parking lot, Ali went into serious training at his Pennsylvania mountain camp. For two months he worked as hard as he had ever done in his life and trimmed down to 15 st. 7½ lb., his lowest weight since taking the title from George Foreman in 1974.

Eight years younger than Ali at 30, Holmes was in his prime at 15 st. 1½ lb. He had ascended to the World Boxing Association throne in 1978 by narrowly outpointing Ken Norton and had since defended the title seven times, winning each bout inside the distance, which equalled a record set by Joe Louis.

Holmes, born in Georgia on 3 November 1949, and raised in Easton, Pennsylvania, had been a professional since March 1973, following an impressive amateur career. He was carefully groomed for world championship honours, winning 27 contests before seeking title recognition. I have become a Larry Holmes fan, and I believe time will prove that he has been the most underrated heavyweight champion in history. He is not only an excellent ring technician and a solid puncher with either fist but is also the most dignified champion since Joe Louis. He has been a credit to boxing with his conduct both inside and outside the ring.

His talent was submerged in the backwash left behind by that quick-on-the-jaw salesman Ali. A quiet, devoted family man, he has suffered by comparison with Ali's overpowering personality and because he's been content to let his boxing do the talking for him he has not been given the projection his ring skills have deserved.

Holmes has proved time and time again that he has got courage to go with his ability. That murderously hard puncher Earnie Shavers knocked him down with the sort of right-hand blow that would have ended most fights. Holmes dragged himself off the canvas and battled back to stop his dangerous opponent in 11 rounds. He was also floored in a title defence against Renaldo Snipes but again got up to win in the 11th. Several times, as against Ken Norton and Mike Weaver, fights were slipping away from him until he dug down into his reserves to show the sort of spirit and determination that sets champions apart from those who only get to challenge.

Holmes was on a hiding to nothing against Ali in Las Vegas. If he won, everybody would say he had beaten a man way past his peak. If he lost, he would be dismissed as having been a mediocre champion. My heart wanted Ali to win but my head said that Holmes would be too young and strong for him. I would have been much happier if Ali had stayed retired after his revenge victory over Leon Spinks. You can go to the well only so many times and I knew that even Ali would have to dry up at some time.

Yet because of the legend that is Ali there was an air of expectancy about his bid to become world champion for a fourth time. Could he produce just one more miracle?

The Fight

Ali *looked* the part for his championship challenge. He was so lean and fit that it was almost as if the clock had been turned back five or six years. But from the very first round it was obvious that Ali's looks were deceiving. Age had robbed him of the speed that used to be his trademark. His quickstep

157

dancing was slowed to a funeral march and the hands that had been so fast now moved as if on a rusted chain.

Holmes produced a performance of near perfection but he got little appreciation because Ali was such a sad shadow of his old self. All that Ali revealed that could be admired was his courage in sticking in there long after it was obvious that Holmes had him licked. No matter what Ali tried, Holmes had an answer for him. He was beating him to the jab, moving quicker around the ring and trapping him by cleverly angling into positions to cut off the challenger's escape routes.

When Ali attempted the rope-a-dope tricks that had worked so well against Foreman, Holmes belted him to the ribs with long hooks that reached around his guard. It was tragic to watch as Ali was virtually reduced to the role of a sparring partner. Even the most biased Ali supporters struggled to score a single round for him, and the man who had so often boasted – with some justification – that he was 'the prettiest' developed an ugly red patch and swelling under his left eye where the champion's jabs were landing with a thumping regularity.

There was just a flash of the old Ali at the start of the fifth round. He came out on his toes and caught Holmes with a couple of stinging lefts to the face. But his legs quickly turned to lead and by the middle of the round he was flat footed as Holmes attacked with both fists to the head and body. The champion was so confident that he was clowning Ali-style, pretending to stagger on the few occasions when the challenger landed a worthwhile punch.

From the seventh round on Ali was surviving on sheer will-power. He seemed to have aged ten years since the first bell and the fierce afternoon heat – it was 104 degrees at the ringside – was taking its toll along with the punishment that Holmes was handing out in a systematic, thoroughly professional manner.

It got to the stage where Holmes was getting sick and tired

of hitting his old hero. 'Why don't you quit?' he kept pleading during clinches.

Ali just said in response: 'Fight, sucker, fight.'

In the eighth round Holmes landed a succession of clubbing rights to Ali's head without reply and in my opinion the referee should have stopped it there and then because Ali was offering no resistance. Ringsiders openly wept as the once mighty Ali stumbled back to his corner with little knowledge of where or who he was. Anybody else but Ali would have surrendered but his stubborn pride wouldn't allow it.

Trainer Angelo Dundee wanted to pull Ali out at the end of the punishing ninth round but others in the challenger's entourage objected. Holmes, a compassionate champion, was clearly holding back in the tenth round and kept inviting referee Richard Green to stop it.

Ali looked a pitiful figure and, as he slumped onto his stool at the end of the round, there was an undignified scuffle between Angelo Dundee, determined to save Ali further humiliation, and Ali's loud-mouthed soulmate Bundini Brown who was demanding 'just one more round'. Thank goodness it was Dundee's commonsense that swayed manager Herbert Muhammad. He summoned the referee over and announced Ali's retirement.

For the first time in his 20-year professional career, Ali had failed to finish a fight. It was a tragic ending to one of the greatest ring careers in the history of boxing. Well, almost the end. Ali being Ali, he had to have one more fling.

The Aftermath

Holmes, to his great credit, did not crow over his victory. He was close to genuine tears of sorrow for Ali and said: 'I love that man. I held back for the whole of the tenth round because I didn't want to see him getting hurt. The referee should have stopped it. He's my friend, my brother. I've got no happiness out of beating him. All I've achieved is a big pay-day. But I ain't celebrating. He's the best heavyweight fighter in the world and just the fact that he was going for the title for a fourth time is a great achievement.

'He tried his old tricks, hoping to pysche me out of it but I got to know him too well during four years as his sparring partner. Ali fooled a few of the writers into thinking he could win. But he couldn't fool me. I hope he never fights again. But nobody can tell Ali what he can or can't do.'

The next day Ali, his damaged eye hidden behind dark glasses, conceded that the fight should have been stopped. 'I was taking a lot of punches and was glad when they stopped it,' he admitted. 'Take your hearts out and turn them over to Larry. He's the heavyweight champion – until I return.'

Ali listened to all the advice of people telling him he should retire and then ignored them all. He foolishly had one more fight, a meaningless affair aginst Canadian Trevor Berbick in the Bahamas in December 1981. At his peak he would hardly have allowed Berbick to lay a glove on him. But a pathetic, lumbering Ali was outpointed over ten mauling rounds and this at last convinced him that his days as 'The Greatest' were well and truly over. A light had gone out on the boxing stage and it will be a long, long time before we see one burning so brightly again.

Ali has since suffered from ill health, no doubt many of his problems being attributable to the fact that he wanted to conquer one mountain too many. He did me the honour of attending my 50th birthday party in London in 1984 and I would be lying if I didn't admit to being shocked and saddened by his appearance. There was a slur to his speech, he had the movements of an old man and there were times when he could hardly keep his eyes open (maybe that was something to do with my boring company!). Obviously the punches he had taken over the years had caught up with him but there were other factors that would need a doctor's diagnosis rather than mine.

The busybody boxing abolitionists would like to convince us that his poor health was all down to his ring career, but his diabetes and liquid-level problems could have afflicted him regardless of what he did for a living. And what he chose to do – boxing – brought him the sort of fame, fortune and sheer satisfaction that he could have found in hardly any other field.

I prefer to remember him as the cocky yet likeable showman of the sixties when he brought a hurricane of fresh air to boxing with his quick wit, twinkling toes and fast fists. During a 60-fight, 20-year career he transcended sport and became the best-known face – and voice – in the world. He was up there with the presidents and kings for instant recognition and was more popular than any of them. I will always harbour a soft spot for him and consider it a privilege to have twice shared the same ring with him.

There is no doubt that for a span of more than a decade he really was 'The Greatest'.

For the Record

Larry Holmes

Born Cuthbert, Georgia, 3 November 1949.
Ht.: 6 ft. 4 in. Wt.: 15 st. 12 lb.
Turned professional 1973. Managed for a time by Richie Giachetti.
Honours: undefeated world heavyweight champion 1978–85.
Record: 47 fights, 47 wins; 34 inside-the-distance wins (7 KOs).

20
The Fight: Larry Holmes v. Gerry Cooney
The Date: 11 June 1982
The Venue: Caesar's Palace, Las Vegas

The Build-up

Nothing stirs the imagination and interest of the boxing public quite as much as a white heavyweight hope. This is in no way meant to be interpreted as a racialist comment but it's box-office fact that the fans will fill any stadium where a white heavyweight is showing signs of power and promise. The Americans reckoned they had unveiled a genuine white hope in Gerry Cooney, a giant 6 ft. 6 in. Irish-American from Long Island, New York.

There had not been a white world heavyweight champion since Ingemar Johansson's brief reign in 1959. Cooney was being touted as the man with the ammunition and the ambition to end the monopoly by black heavyweights. There was just one slight problem. Larry Holmes was standing in his way.

Cooney had hurried into the No.1 contender's slot with 25 wins in 25 starts, and only three of his opponents had been around to hear the final bell. He was destroying all opposition with what had been my favourite punch, a left hook that he reckoned was guaranteed to put the lights out if it landed on target. There were plenty of cynics around quick to point to the fact that Cooney had got to the top of the ratings on the backs of a procession of over-the-hill opponents. But there is hardly ever a heavyweight championship prospect who doesn't face this sort of accusation at some stage in his career.

Because of a run of back and shoulder injuries, Cooney had only two fights in the 20 months leading up to the showdown with Holmes. Both were short and savage affairs that revealed his explosive power. He blasted out highly regarded Ron Lyle in just two and a half minutes in October 1980, and then seven months later took just 54 seconds to dispose of veteran Ken Norton who had been in with the very best and had no doubt left a lot of his appetite behind him. Even so, the merciless manner in which Cooney destroyed Norton was a warning to Holmes that his challenge had to be treated with deadly seriousness.

Cooney, born in Huntington, New York, on 24 August 1956, was one of six children fathered by Tony Cooney, an Irish-American ironworker who made his living helping to build and recondition the New York skyscrapers. His son, Gerry, was something of a skyscraper even as a youngster and towered over kids his own age. Tony Cooney was a boxing and fitness fantatic and introduced his four sons to boxing in the hope that one of them would fulfil his dream of raising a world champion.

He built a makeshift ring in the backyard and encouraged his four boys to spar among themselves and also with neighbouring children. Gerry showed the most potential and his father perhaps pushed him too hard, getting him up at 5.30 every morning for exercises and road runs and insisting on early nights. Gerry rebelled against the strict discipline and left home to live with an elder brother. When his father died of cancer in 1975 Gerry took to boxing seriously as a show of respect.

'I owe my father so much,' he said during the build-up to the Holmes fight. 'I didn't really appreciate that he was trying to give me the right sort of discipline when I was a kid. It's only now that I understand what he was doing. I just wish he was here to see the result of the great foundation that he laid for me.'

He had a special green (of course) dressing-gown made and embroidered over a large shamrock were the words Gerry, Dad and Mom. 'I want to win the title for the Cooney family,' he said.

As with many good left-hookers (I immodestly include myself in that league), Cooney started out as a southpaw but was switched to orthodox when he began boxing with the local YMCA club. He was spotted – at 6 ft. 6 in. and 16 st. he could hardly be missed – by two noisy newcomers to the boxing management scene, Dennis Rappaport and Mike Jones.

They signed him as a professional in 1977 and steered him on a carefully plotted course towards championship contention. Rappaport and Jones were like a double act out of the pages of a Damon Runyan 'Guys and Dolls' yarn and filled acres of newspaper space and television and radio time with verbal publicity pumps for Cooney.

Here are a couple of gems from their vast repetoire of Cooneyisms:

Rappaport: 'Gerry has the good looks and the charm of an Irish tenor, the humility and graciousness of a Victorian maiden. Many people can readily identify with him.'

Jones: 'Gerry has the potential to make $50 million from endorsements and advertising once he has got the title. He's got everything going for him. He'll not only be the champion of the world but also the champion of Wall Street.'

The question was: could Cooney provide action to go with the words of his brash managers?

The championship fight was originally scheduled for March but was postponed for three months when Cooney ripped a

164

muscle in his left shoulder. The postponement angered Holmes who stepped out of character when he said: 'The injury is in his mind. Cooney's a looney and is frightened stiff of me. If he wasn't white, he'd be dismissed as just another fighter. He wants to hide behind his ma's apron. All he's done is postpone his punishment.'

It was so unlike Holmes to resort to such personal insults that I could only guess he was doing it to keep the box-office managers happy. Champion and challenger had been guaranteed $10 million each and promoter Don King was looking to collect $60 million from world-wide closed-circuit television alone. Somebody had to bang the publicity drum and I reckon Holmes – a Larry the Lamb outside the ring – was having words put into his mouth to boost ticket sales.

Holmes went into the fight in a mean mood. He did not feel that he was getting the recognition he deserved as world champion, mainly because he was still having to live in the long shadow cast by that living legend Muhammad Ali. He had no doubt that he could win.

His confidence had been boosted by 11 successful championship defences and he said dismissively of Cooney: 'He'll go in seven – sooner if he gets cocky. The fight will end when I want it to end. I'm going to move real quick around that ring and make him drunk before I mug him. I'm an executive boxer, not ordinary like Cooney. He's never been in the ring with anyone like me. What's he going to do when the punches are coming at him at a hundred miles an hour? He's too big a target to miss. He ain't the Great White Hope. He's the Great White Hype.'

It was like listening to a Muhammad Ali script but it didn't carry quite the same entertainment value coming from Holmes, who talks with a lisp and with a lot less decibels than when Ali was trumpeting his ticket-sales talk.

Cooney tried to play down the black v. white talk that gave an undesirable racial undertone to the pre-fight spiel. 'Holmes has brought up the black-against-white thing too many times,' said Cooney. 'It doesn't matter if your skin is white, black or green. You should only be judged on your boxing.'

He added with grim determination: 'I'm going into the ring to win. This fight means more than money to me. I want that championship for my dad.'

The Fight

This was a world heavyweight title fight that lived up to its billing. They called it 'The Pride and the Glory'. Cooney provided the pride, Holmes the glory. In fact there was pride *and* glory for Holmes. He produced a mesmerising performance that made many sceptics reassess his ability and he was at last accepted as being one of the truly great champions.

A lot was made before the fight about how Cooney, a devastating body-puncher, planned to break the champion's ribs with his brutalizing left hooks. The challenger spent all the time during the referee's pre-fight instructions staring at Holmes's stomach, trying to chill the champion with the thought of his body punches.

Unfortunately for Cooney, Holmes had a fight plan of his own that didn't allow for closequarter exchanges. He dictated the pattern of the fight from arm's length, jabbing his left through Cooney's poorly constructed defence almost at will. The champion circled away from Cooney's much-publicized left hook and when the challenger attempted to throw it with full force in round two he coolly stepped inside and drilled a right counter to the jaw. The challenger took four steps backwards on suddenly rubberized legs and fell into a sitting position in the champion's corner.

He was up at four and managed to cover up against an all-out attack after taking the mandatory eight count. It was then that Cooney's great pride came into play. It looked to most ringsiders as if Holmes was in for an easy defence of his title but this wasn't allowing for Gerry's fighting instincts.

He took the fight to Holmes in the third round as he became a towering inferno and the champion was on the receiving end of some heavy left hooks that forced him to seek the shelter of a clinch. Cooney then banged away to the body for the first time with real effect and by the end of the third and fourth rounds he had earned the respect of both the champion and the millions of spectators watching the fight around the world.

Holmes for a while there was looking every minute of his 33 years, while Cooney, 25, was calling on the strength of youth. But confidence in an upset victory by the brave Irish-American started to evaporate in the sixth round after he had walked into the same sort of right counter that had dropped him in the second.

This time he managed to stay on his feet but his senses had been scrambled and Holmes followed up with a vicious right uppercut that sent the challenger's gumshield flying.

From then on Cooney was in the fight only as a supporting actor to the undisputed star, Larry Holmes. Cooney proved he had a giant heart but clearly did not have the experience or ring craft to put the champion out of his smooth stride. In desperation, Cooney started throwing punches from all angles and several landed low. There was a no foul rule in operation so the challenger escaped with severe warnings for tactics that were not deliberately dirty but the last resort of a heavily outgunned fighter. He was just hitting and hoping rather than aiming below the belt on purpose.

Bleeding heavily from a gashed nose, Cooney swung a wild punch in the ninth round that landed so low that the champion was in danger of being kneecapped; although to be honest another part of his anatomy was in greater danger than his knees. Holmes doubled over with pain and took two and a half minutes to recover before referee Mills Lane waved them back into fierce action.

The tenth round was a toe-to-toe war and I sensed it was something of a final fling from Cooney who had never gone more than nine rounds before. The 11th and 12th rounds were living nightmares for the challenger as Holmes, superbly conditioned by experienced trainer Eddie Futch, somehow stepped up his pace and started driving in two-fisted combination punches.

Cooney was so far gone in the 13th that Holmes was measuring him with his left before teeing off with mighty right hands that continually rocked the fading white hope. He was sagging helplessly on the ropes with the referee about to give him a standing count when Cooney's veteran trainer Victor Valle – breaking the rules of boxing – scrambled into the ring and cuddled the challenger to him. 'That's enough ref!' Valle shouted. 'I love this guy. I don't want him taking anymore.'

After the official verdict – a disqualification – had been announced, an emotional Cooney took the microphone and said in a faltering voice: 'I tried with all my heart. I love you. I'm sorry. I'm sorry that I've let people down.' Then, weeping, he returned to his corner unaware that the crowd were on their feet cheering his words. He didn't owe anybody any apologies.

It had been a magnificent show of defiance by the challenger, and an even more magnificent display of controlled box-fighting by a *great* champion. Dare I say that it was an ideal Holmes exhibition? No, perhaps I'd better not. Just suffice to say that Holmes had proved beyond argument that he was a world heavyweight champion to rank with the very best in history.

The Aftermath

There was no bitterness or recrimination after the fight. Holmes defused the black-against-white situation by saying: 'I didn't fight this fight for the blacks, the whites or the Spanish. I fought this fight for the people. We're all God's children. I don't see colour. I'm not a racist. When I look at

Gerry Cooney I just see a man trying to take my head off. Don't matter what colour he is. I've just got to get to him and do my job.'

He looked towards Cooney and said: 'I want to compliment Gerry Cooney. I think he's a great fighter. I shook his hand before the fight and I shook his hand after the fight.'

'Larry is the champion,' said Cooney. 'No question. There's no bitterness. I guess I had not had enough action before getting into the ring. Two rounds of boxing in 20 months is not the right preparation to face a fighter as good as Holmes. I was rusty. But I'll have everything right the next time.'

There was never a next time. Gerry appeared to have had his love of fighting knocked out of him by his one and only defeat until a gently paced comeback in 1984 started to take shape and he was once again looking the brightest of the white hopes.

Holmes announced the end of his distinguished career after his 47th victory in his 47th fight against David Bey in Las Vegas on 15 March 1985. But the chance of beating Rocky Marciano's all-time record of 49 victories in 49 fights was too strong a magnet. He returned to the ring to outpoint Carl 'The Truth' Williams over 15 tough rounds and the eyes of the boxing world were trained on him as he made plans to try to stretch his unbeaten run to 50 fights.

Everybody recognizes Holmes as the King, even though he surrendered the WBC version of the championship rather than be pressured into taking fights he didn't want for purses that didn't suit his pocket. As I write, he has made 19 successful defences of his crown, not including the one-round destruction of Marvis Frazier which was not sanctioned as a title fight.

Holmes has financial security for life, a thriving hotel business and a happy family. He has given a lot to the sport and must now go down as one of the all-time greats. Had he followed anybody but Ali as champion he would have long ago gained recognition as one of the heavyweight masters.

Boxing and Larry Holmes have been very good to each other. Holmes Sweet Holmes!

For the Record

Gerry Cooney

Born Huntington, New York, 24 August 1956.
Ht.: 6 ft. 6 in. Wt.: 16 st.
Turned professional 1977. Managed by Dennis Rappaport and
  Mike Jones.
Record: 26 fights, 25 wins, 1 loss (no KOs); 23 inside-the-distance
  wins (18 KOs).

21

The Computer Versus Henry Cooper

Norman Giller, the writer who has helped me get my scrap-book memories down on paper, is a computer freak who fed all the facts and figures on every 20th-century British heavyweight champion into a computer to find who has been the greatest. This is how his final top ten table looked after the computer had digested all the data:

	Ht.	Wt.	Fights	Wins	Losses	TKOs	KOs	KO'd	Total Rounds
1 Tommy Farr	6–1	14–6	104	71	22	12	11	1	995
2 Bruce Woodcock	6–½	13–1	38	34	4	22	10	1	192
3 Joe Bugner	6–4	16–0	70	58	11	39	6	1	461
4 Henry Cooper	6–2	13–9	55	40	14	20	7	4	362
5 Don Cockell	5–10	14–9	79	64	14	17	20	3	506
6 Jack Petersen	6–1½	12–12	38	33	5	10	11	0	292
7 Len Harvey	6–00	12–12	133	111	13	34	22	1	1232
8 Billy Wells	6–3	13–8	52	41	11	8	27	11	335
9 Joe Erskine	6–½	14.0	53	44	8	12	2	1	425
10 Joe Beckett	5–10	14–8	51	41	10	14	16	5	295

It makes me fighting mad to see myself rated below Joe Bugner. I'm convinced he would not have lived with me at my peak. And I'm also sure that everybody else listed in this table would have got the better of him if they had met when at their best. Len Harvey was one of the all-time greats and I queried with 'Know-all Norm' why he is so low in the table. Apparently his bodyweight was against him. His best years were in the light-heavyweight division.

I don't usually get drawn into the ratings lark because I feel any champion can only be the best of his era. But I believe I am better qualified than a computer to rate the top post-war British heavyweights. The computer can't take *feelings* into account to go with the cold facts and figures. This would be my top ten British table. It includes only post-war boxers whom I have either fought or seen in the flesh:

1 Joe Erskine (Wales)
2 Bruce Woodcock (England)
3 Don Cockell (England)
4 Joe Bugner (England)
5 Frank Bruno (England)
6 Brian London (England)
7 Dick Richardson (Wales)
8 Jack Bodell (England)
9 Johnny Williams (Wales)
10 Billy Walker (England)
   Johnny Prescott (England)

I am watching Frank Bruno's rise with interest. In my opinion too many of his matches have been of the no-risk variety, but in manager Terry Lawless's shoes I suppose I would have brought him along at a similar pace. There is a stiffness about him that worries me but there is no question that he has natural punching power that will always keep him in with a chance when the going gets tough. He has certainly got all the equipment but I reserve final judgement on him until I see him in action against the top Yanks. Only then will we know his true potential.

Here's how Norman's computer rated the top ten world heavyweight champions of the last 50 years – from 1935 when 'Cinderella Man' James J. Braddock was on the throne:

		Ht.	Wt.	Fights	Wins	Losses	TKOs	KOs	KO'd	Total Rounds
1	Rocky Marciano	5–10½	13–2	49	49	0	43	32	0	243
2	Joe Louis	6–1½	14–6	71	68	3	55	43	1	444
3	Muhammad Ali	6–3	16–0	61	56	5	37	29	0	540
4	Larry Holmes	6–½	15–12	48	48	0	34	7	0	350
5	Sonny Liston	6–1	15–4	54	50	4	39	25	2	270
6	George Foreman	6–3½	15–12	47	45	2	42	27	1	152
7	Joe Frazier	5–11½	14–6	36	32	4	27	10	0	203
8	Joe Walcott	6–0	13–12	67	49	17	31	29	6	468
9	Floyd Patterson	6–0	13–6	64	55	8	40	16	2	417
10	Ingo Johansson	6–½	14–0	28	26	2	18	11	2	175

The eye-opener for me is that Ali boxed nearly 100 rounds more than Joe Louis, and even more than Jersey Joe Walcott whose career spanned 23 years. And remember that right at what should have been the peak of his career Ali had three-and-a-half years out of action because of his dispute with the US government over his refusal to join the army and fight in Vietnam.

Using my feelings as well as facts as a guide and taking each fighter at his very best, my top ten world heavyweight champions for the last fifty years would be:

1 =	Joe Louis
	Muhammad Ali
3	Rocky Marciano
4	Larry Holmes
5	George Foreman
6	Sonny Liston
7	Joe Frazier
8	Jersey Joe Walcott
9	Floyd Patterson
10	Ingemar Johansson

Sorry to chicken out over the No. 1 spot but I honestly cannot bring myself to separate Louis and Ali. Both, at the peak of their powers, had equal claims to being called 'The Greatest'. I believe that at their best both would have had the ring craft and the power to outmanoeuvre Rocky Marciano.

Ali and Marciano were matched in a computer fight shortly before Rocky's death in a plane crash in 1969. They simulated seven different finishes and when the film was released two weeks after Rocky's funeral it showed Marciano winning by a tenth-round knockout.

But Ali told me some time later: 'The whole thing was a sham. It was phony from start to finish and neither Rocky nor I were happy with the way it was done. He was a great champion but the way he fought – you know, taking three or four punches to land one – he would never have been able to defend the title as often and as regularly as I did.'

It's difficult to argue with Rocky's perfect 49-fights, 49 victories record, but he defended the championship only six times before he retired and his legend of invincibility was built against once-retired 37-year-old Joe Louis, twice-retired 38-year-old Jersy Joe Walcott, 40-year-old Archie Moore and 34-year-old Ezzard Charles who had left his best behind him. I don't want to take anything away from Rocky. He was great for boxing, but I have to pick Louis and Ali ahead of him because I feel they were better all-round ring generals who would have come up with a strategy to beat him.

I know my opinions will start more arguments than they will settle, but that's what helps to make boxing such a compelling sport. It's great for conversation and nostalgia as well as action. I hope you've enjoyed taking a ringside seat with me and that some of my scrapbook memories have helped revive memorable boxing moments for you. Thanks for being in my corner.

Appendix
All the World Heavyweight Champions

Their births, weights, full records and title defences, compiled by Norman Giller.

John L. Sullivan
Born Roxbury, Mass., 15 October 1858
Died Abingdon, Mass., 2 February 1918
Ht.: 5 ft. 10 in. Wt.: 13 st. 6 lb.
Reach: 74 in. Chest: 43–48 in. Fist: 14 in.
Nickname: The Boston Strong Boy
Career span: 1878–1905
Record: 75 fights, 31 wins, 16 KOs*, 3 draws, 1 loss (KO'd), 40 no decisions**
Age at which title was won: 34, in his 13th fight

Sullivan took the title from Irishman Paddy Ryan with a ninth-round knock-out at Mississippi City on 2 February 1892.

Championship defences:
10.3.88 drew 39 rounds Charlie Mitchell (GB) at Chantilly, France
8.8.89 w.rsf. 75 Jake Kilrain (USA) at Richburg, Mass.***
7.9.92 1.KO.21 James J. Corbett (USA) at New Orleans

*KOs as in the American interpretation, i.e. a stoppage of any kind
**'No decision' contests were introduced to beat a boxing ban when only exhibitions were allowed. Ringside reporters used to judge who had won.
***Last bare-knuckle championship fight.

James J. Corbett

Born San Francisco, 1 September 1866
Died Bayside, Long Island, 18 February 1933
Ht.: 6 ft. 1 in. Wt.: 13 st.
Reach: 73 in. Chest: 38–42 in. Fist: 12¾ in.
Nickname: Gentleman Jim
Career span: 1884–1903
Record: 33 fights, 20 wins (9 KOs), 6 draws, 5 losses (KO'd 3), 2
  no decisions
Age at which title was won: 26, in his 25th fight

Championship defences:
25.1.94 w.KO.3 Charlie Mitchell (GB) at Jacksonville
17.3.97 l.KO.14 Bob Fitzsimmons (GB, naturalized US) at Carson
City

Bob Fitzsimmons

Born Helston, Cornwall, 4 June 1862
Died Chicago, 22 October 1917
Ht.: 5 ft. 11¾ in. Wt.: 11 st. 8 lb.
Reach: 71¾ in. Chest: 41–44 in. Fist: 12½ in.
Nicknames: Ruby Robert and Freckled Bob
Career span: 1880–1914
Record: 41 fights, 28 wins (23 KOs), 1 draw, 7 losses (KO'd 6), 5
  no decisions
He also won the world middle and light-heavyweight titles
Age at which heavyweight title was won: 35, in his 23rd fight

Championship defence:
9.6.99 l.KO.11 James J. Jeffries (USA) at Coney Island

James J. Jeffries

Born Caroll, Ohio, 15 April 1875
Died Burbank, California, 3 March 1953
Ht.: 6 ft. 2½ in. Wt.: 15 st. 7 lb.
Reach: 76½ in. Chest: 43–48½ in. Fist: 13½ in.
Nicknames: The Boilermaker and Californian Grizzly Bear
Career span: 1896–1910
Record: 23 fights, 20 wins (16 KOs), 2 draws, 1 loss (KO'd)
Age at which title was won: 24, in his 13th fight

Championship defences:
 3.11.99 w.pts.25 Tom Sharkey (Ire) at Coney Island
11.5.00 w.KO.23 James J. Corbett (USA) at Coney Island
15.11.01 w.ret.5 Gus Ruhlin (USA) at San Francisco
25.7.02 w.KO.8 Bob Fitzsimmons (GB) at San Francisco
14.8.03 w.KO.10 James J. Corbett (USA) at San Francisco
26.8.04 w.KO.2 Jack Munro (USA) at San Francisco

(Jeffries announced his retirement and nominated Marvin Hart and Jack Root to fight for the vacant title on 3 July 1905 at Reno, Nevada. Hart won on a 12th-round stoppage.)

Marvin Hart

Born Jefferson County, Kentucky, 16 September, 1876
Died Fern Creek, Kentucky, 17 September 1931
Ht.: 5 ft. 11¼ in. Wt.: 13 st. 5 lb.
Career span: 1899–1910
Record: 48 fights, 29 wins (20 KOs), 4 draws, 7 losses (KO'd 4), 8 no decisions
Age at which title was won: 28, in his 36th fight

Championship defence
23.2.06 l.pts. 20 Tommy Burns (Canada) at Los Angeles

Tommy Burns

Real name Noah Brusso
Born Chesley, Ontario, 17 June 1881
Died Vancouver, 10 May 1955
Ht.: 5 ft. 7 in. Wt.: 12 st. 5 lb.
Reach: 74½ in. Chest: 40–43¾ in. Fist: 12 in.
Career span: 1900–1920
Record: 60 fights, 46 wins (36 KOs), 8 draws, 5 losses (KO'd 1), 1 no decision
Age at which title was won: 25, in his 39th fight

Championship defences:
 2.10.06 w.KO.15 Jim Flynn (USA) at Los Angeles
28.11.06 drew 20 Philadelphia Jack O'Brien (USA) at Los Angeles
 8.5.07 w.pts. 20 Philadelphia Jack O'Brien (USA) at Los Angeles
 4.7.07 w.KO.1 Bill Squires (Aus) at Colma, California
 2.12.07 w.KO.10 Gunner Moir (GB) at London

10.2.08   w.KO.4 Jack Palmer (GB) at London
17.3.08   w.KO.1 Jem Roche (Ire) at Dublin
18.4.08   w.KO.5 Jewey Smith (GB) at Paris
13.6.08   w.KO.13 Bill Squires (Aus) at Paris
24.8.08   w.KO.13 Bill Squires (Aus) at Sydney
 2.9.08 w.KO.6 Bill Lang (Aus) at Melbourne
26.12.08 1.rsf.14 Jack Johnson (USA) at Sydney

Jack Johnson

Born Galveston, Texas, 31 March 1878
Died Raleigh, North Carolina, 10 June 1946
Ht.: 6 ft. ¼ in. Wt.: 13 st 10lbs.
Reach: 74 in. Chest: 37½–42¾ in. Fist: 14 in.
Nicknames: Li'l Artha and The Galveston Giant
Career span: 1897–1928
Record: 113 fights, 78 wins (44 KOs), 14 draws, 7 losses (KO'd 5),
    14 no decisions
Age at which title was won: 30, in his 76th fight

Championship defences:
16.10.09 w.KO.12 Stanley Ketchel (USA) at Colma, California
 4.7.10   w.rsf.15 James J. Jeffries (USA) at Reno, Nevada
 4.7.12   w.rsf.9 Jim Flynn (USA) at Las Vegas
28.11.13 w.KO.2 André Spoul (Fra) at Paris
19.12.13 drew 10 Jim Johnson (USA) at Paris
27.6.14   w.pts. 20 Frank Moran (USA) at Paris
 5.4.15   1.KO.26 Jess Willard (USA) at Havana

Jess Willard

Born Pottawatomie County, Kansas, 29 December 1881
Died Los Angeles, 15 December 1968
Ht.: 6 ft. 6¼ in. Wt.: 17 st. 8 lb.
Reach: 83 in. Chest: 46–49½ in. Fist: 14 in.
Nickname: The Pottawatomie Giant
Career span: 1911–1923
Record: 36 fights, 24 wins (20 KOs), 1 draw, 6 losses (KO'd 2), 5
    no decisions
Age at which title was won: 33, in his 31st fight

Championship defences
25.3.16   no decision 10 Frank Moran (USA) at New York
 4.7.19   l.ret.3 Jack Dempsey (USA) at Toledo

Jack Dempsey

Born Manassa, Colorado, 24 June 1895
Died New York, 31 May 1983
Ht.: 6 ft. 1 in. Wt.: 13 st. 4 lb.
Reach: 77 in. Chest: 42–46 in. Fist: 11¼ in.
Nicknames: Manassa Mauler and Idol of Fistiana
Career span: 1914–1940
Record: 81 fights, 60 wins (49 KOs), 8 draws, 7 losses (KO'd 1),
   6 no decisions
Age at which title was won: 24, in about his 73rd fight (he had
many unrecorded contests)

Championship defences
 6.9.20   w.KO.3 Billy Miske (USA) at Benton Harbour
14.12.20   w.KO.12 Bill Brennan (USA) at New York
 2.7.21   w.KO.4 Georges Carpentier (Fra) at Jersey City
 4.7.23   w.pts. 15 Tom Gibbons (USA) at Shelby, Montana
14.9.23   w.KO.2 Luis Angel Firpo (Arg) at New York
23.9.26   l.pts.10 Gene Tunney (USA) at Philadelphia

Gene Tunney

Born New York City, 25 May 1898
Died Greenwich, Connecticut, 7 November 1978
Ht.: 6 ft. ½ in. Wt.: 13 st. 5 lb.
Reach: 77 in. Chest: 42–45 in. Fist: 11¼ in.
Nickname: The Fighting Marine
Career span: 1915–1928
Record: 76 fights, 56 wins (41 KOs), 1 draw, 1 loss, 17 no decisions,
   1 dnc*
His one defeat was a points loss to Harry Greb in a light-heavy-
weight bout
Age at which title was won: 28, in his 74th fight

Championship defences
22.9.27   w.pts. 10 Jack Dempsey (USA) at Chicago
23.7.28   w.rsf.11 Tom Heeney (NZ) at New York

*Dnc = declared no contest

(Tunney retired as undefeated champion. German Max Schmeling beat Jack Sharkey on a fourth-round disqualification to win the vacant title on 12 June, 1930 at New York.)

Max Schmeling

Born Klein Luckaw, Brandenburg, Germany, 28 September 1905
Ht.: 6 ft. 1 in. Wt.: 13 st. 4 lb.
Reach: 76 in. Chest: 43–47 in. Fist: 12 in.
Nickname: Black Uhlan
Career span: 1924–1948
Record: 71 fights, 56 wins (39 KOs), 5 draws, 10 losses (KO'd 5)
Age at which title was won: 24, in his 51st fight

Championship defences
  3.7.31 w.rsf.15 Young Stribling (USA) at Cleveland
21.6.32 l.pts.15 Jack Sharkey (USA) at Long Island

Jack Sharkey

Original name Joseph Paul Zukauskas
Born Binghamton, New York, 6 October 1902
Ht.: 6 ft. Wt.: 14 st. 6 lb.
Reach: 74½ in. Chest 40½–45½ in. Fist: 12¾ in.
Nicknames: Boston Cob and Sobbing Sailor
Career span: 1924–1936
Record: 55 fights, 38 wins (15 KOs), 3 draws, 13 losses (KO'd 4),
  1 no decision
Age at which title was won: 29, in his 47th fight

Championship defence
29.6.33 l.KO.6 Primo Carnera (Italy) at Long Island

Primo Carnera

Born Sequals, Italy, 26 October 1906
Died Sequals, 29 June 1967 (on 34th anniversary of his title win)
Ht.: 6 ft. 5¾ in. Wt.: 18 st. 6 lb.
Reach: 85½ in. Chest: 48–54 in. Fist: 14¾ in.
Nickname: The Amblin Alp
Career span: 1928–1945
Record: 99 fights, 86 wins (66 KOs), 12 losses (KO'd 6), 1 dnc
Age at which title was won: 26, in his 82nd fight

Championship defences
22.10.33 w.pts.15 Paulino Uzcudun (Spain) at Rome
 1.3.34 w.pts.15 Tommy Loughran (USA) at Miami
14.6.34 l.rsf.11 Max Baer (USA) at Long Island

Max Baer

Born Omaha, Nebraska, 11 February 1909
Died Hollywood, 21 November 1959
Ht.: 6 ft. 2½ in. Wt.: 15 st.
Reach: 81 in. Chest: 44–47½ in. Fist: 12 in.
Nicknames: The Livermore Larruper and Madcap Maxie
Career span: 1929–1941
Record: 79 fights, 65 wins (50 KOs), 13 losses (KO'd 3), 1 no
  decision
Age at which title was won: 25, in his 48th fight

Championship defence
13.6.35 l.pts.15 James J. Braddock (USA) at Long Island

James J. Braddock

Born New York City, 6 December 1905
Died New Jersey, 29 November 1974
Ht.: 6 ft. 2½ in. Wt.: 13 st. 8 lb.
Reach: 75 in. Chest: 41–44 in. Fist: 11½ in.
Nickname: Cinderella Man
Career span: 1926–1938
Record: 85 fights, 51 wins (26 KOs), 3 draws, 22 losses (KO'd 2),
  7 no decisions, 2 dnc
Age at which title was won: 29, in his 83rd fight

Championship defence
22.6.37 l.KO.8 Joe Louis (USA) at Chicago

Joe Louis

Original name Joe Louis Barrow
Born Lafayette, Alabama, 13 May 1914
Died Las Vegas, 12 April 1981
Ht.: 6 ft. 1½ in. Wt.: 14 st. 2 lb.
Reach: 76 in. Chest: 42–45 in. Fist: 11¾ in.
Nickname: Brown Bomber

Career span: 1934–1951
Record: 71 fights, 68 wins (54 KOs), 3 losses (2 KO'd)
Age at which title was won: 23, in his 36th fight
Defended the title a record 25 times

Championship defences
30.8.37 w.pts.15 Tommy Farr (GB) at New York
23.2.38 w.KO.3 Nathan Mann (USA) at New York
 1.4.38 w.KO.5 Harry Thomas (USA) at Chicago
22.6.38 w.rsf.1 Max Schmeling (GER) at New York
20.5.39 w.rsf.1 John Henry Lewis (USA) at New York
17.4.39 w.KO.1 Jack Roper (USA) at Los Angeles
28.6.39 w.rsf.4 Tony Galento (USA) at New York
20.9.39 w.KO.11 Bob Pastor (USA) at Detroit
 9.2.40 w.pts.15 Arturo Godoy (CHILE) at New York
29.3.40 w.rsf.2 Johnny Paychek (USA) at New York
20.6.40 w.rsf.8 Arturo Godoy (CHILE) at New York
16.12.40 w.ret.6 Al McCoy (CAN) at Boston
31.1.41 w.KO.5 Red Burman (USA) at New York
17.2.41 w.KO.2 Gus Dorazio (USA) at Philadelphia
21.3.41 w.rsf.13 Abe Simon (USA) at Detroit
 8.4.41 w.rsf.9 Tony Musto (USA) at St Louis
23.5.41 w.dis.7 Buddy Baer (USA) at Washington
18.6.41 w.KO.13 Billy Conn (USA) at New York
29.9.41 w.rsf.6 Lou Nova (USA) at New York
 9.1.42 w.KO.1 Buddy Baer (USA) at New York
27.3.42 w.KO.6 Abe Simon (USA) at New York
19.6.46 w.KO.8 Billy Conn (USA) at New York
18.9.46 w.KO.1 Tami Mauriello (USA) at New York
 5.12.47 w.pts.15 Jersey Joe Walcott (USA) at New York
25.6.48 w.KO.11 Jersey Joe Walcott (USA) at New York

(Louis retired. Ezzard Charles became champion by outpointing Jersey Joe Walcott 22 June 1949, in Chicago.)

Ezzard Charles

Born Lawrenceville, Georgia, 7 July 1921
Died Chicago, 27 May 1970
Ht.: 6 ft. Wt.: 13 st.
Reach: 74 in. Chest: 39–42 in. Fist: 12 in.
Nickname: Cincinnati Cobra

My Most Memorable Fights

Career span: 1940–1959
Record: 122 fights, 96 wins (58 KOs), 1 draw, 25 losses (KO'd 7)
Age at which title was won: 29, in his 65th fight

Championship defences
10.8.49   w.rsf.7 Gus Lesnevich (USA) at New York
14.10.49 w.KO.8 Pat Valentino (USA) at San Francisco
15.8.50   w.rsf.14 Freddie Beshore (USA) at Buffalo
27.9.50   w.pts.15 Joe Louis (USA) at New York
 5.12.50 w.KO.11 Nick Barone (USA) at Cincinnati
12.1.51   w.rsf.10 Lee Oma (USA) at New York
 7.3.51   w.pts.15 Jersey Joe Walcott (USA) at Detroit
30.5.51   w.pts.15 Joey Maxim (USA) at Chicago
18.7.51   l.KO.7 Jersey Joe Walcott (USA) at Pittsburgh

Jersey Joe Walcott

Original name Arnold Cream
Born Merchantville, New Jersey, 31 January 1914
Ht.: 6 ft. Wt.: 13 st. 8 lb.
Reach: 74 in. Chest: 40–43 in. Fist: 12 in.
Nickname: Jersey Joe
Career span: 1930–1953
Record: 67 fights, 49 wins (30 KOs), 1 draw, 17 losses (KO'd 6)
Age at which title was won: 37, in about his 64th fight (he had several unrecorded contests) – the oldest to win the championship

Championship defences
 5.6.52   w.pts.15 Ezzard Charles (USA) at Philadelphia
23.9.52   l.KO.13 Rocky Marciano (USA) at Philadelphia

Rocky Marciano

Original name Rocco Francis Marchegiano
Born Brockton, Mass., 1 September 1923
Died in an air crash Newton, Iowa, 31 August 1969
Ht.: 5 ft. 10¼ in. Wt.: 13 st. 2 lb.
Reach: 68 in. Chest: 39–42 in. Fist: 11½ in.
Nickname: Brockton Blockbuster
Record: 49 fights, 49 wins (43 KOs); retired as undefeated champion
Age at which title was won: 29, in his 43rd fight

Championship defences
15.5.53   w.KO.1 Jersey Joe Walcott (USA) at Chicago
24.9.53   w.rsf.11 Roland LaStarza (USA) at New York
17.6.54   w.pts.15 Ezzard Charles (USA) at New York
17.9.54   w.KO.8 Ezzard Charles (USA) at New York
16.5.55   w.rsf. 9 Don Cockell (GB) at San Francisco
21.9.55   w.KO.9 Archie Moore (USA) at New York
(Marciano retired as undefeated champion. Floyd Patterson knocked out Archie Moore in five rounds to win the vacant title on 30 November 1956, at Chicago.)

Floyd Patterson

Born Waco, North Carolina, 4 January 1935
Ht.; 6 ft. Wt.: 13 st. 2 lb.
Reach: 71 in. Chest: 40–42 in. Fist: 12¾ in.
Olympic middleweight champion 1952
Nickname: Freudian Floyd
Career span: 1952–1972
Record: 64 fights, 55 wins (40 KOs), 1 draw, 8 losses (KO'd 5)
Age at which title was won: 21, in his 32nd fight
The youngest champion and the first to regain the title

Championship defences
29.7.57   w.rsf.10 Tommy Jackson (USA) at New York
22.8.57   w.KO.6 Pete Rademacher (USA) at Seattle
18.8.58   w.ret.12 Roy Harris (USA) at Los Angeles
 1.5.59   w.KO.11 Brian London (GB) at Indianapolis
26.6.59   l.rsf.3 Ingemar Johansson (Sweden) at New York

Ingemar Johansson

Born Gothenburg, Sweden, 22 September 1932
Ht.: 6 ft. ½ in. Wt.: 14 st.
Reach: 72½ in. Chest: 43–45 in. Fist: 13½ in.
Nickname (for his right-hand punch): Ingo's Bingo
Career span: 1952–1963
Record: 28 fights, 26 wins, 2 losses (KO'd 2)
Age at which title was won: 26, in his 22nd fight

Championship defences
20.6.60   l.KO.5 Floyd Patterson (USA) at New York
13.3.61   Patterson w.KO.6 Ingemar Johansson (Sweden) at Miami

4.12.61 w.KO.4 Tom McNeeley (USA) at Tornoto
25.9.62 l.KO.1 Sonny Liston (USA) at Chicago

Charles (Sonny) Liston

Born Arkansas, 8 May 1932
Died Las Vegas, 30 December 1970
Ht.: 6 ft. 1 in. Wt.: 15 st. 3 lb.
Reach: 84 in. Chest: 44–46½ in. Fist: 15 in.
Nickname: Old Stone Face
Career span: 1953–1970
Record: 54 fights, 50 wins (39 KOs), 4 losses (KO'd 3)
Age at which title was won: 30, in his 35th fight

Championship defences
22.7.63   w.KO.1 Floyd Patterson (USA) at Las Vegas
25.2.64   l.ret.6 Cassius Clay (USA) at Miami
(Clay was stripped of the title by the WBA for agreeing to a return
fight with Liston. Ernie Terrell (USA) outpointed Eddie Machen
(USA) for the vacant WBA version of the title on 5 March 1965,
at Chicago.)

Muhammad Ali

Originally Cassius Marcellus Clay
Born Louisville, Kentucky, 17 January 1942
Ht.: 6 ft. 3 in. Wt.: 15 st. 10 lb.
Reach: 82 in. Chest: 43–45½ in. Fist: 12½ in.
Nicknames: Louisville Lip and The Greatest
Olympic light-heavyweight champion 1960
Career span: 1960–1981
Record: 61 fights, 56 wins (37 KOs), 5 losses (no KOs)
Age at which he won the title: 22, in his 20th fight
He is the only champion to have won the title three times

Ernie Terrell

Born Inverness, Mississippi, 4 April 1939
Ht.: 6 ft. 6 in. Wt.: 15 st. 4 lb.
Reach: 84 in. Chest: 44½–47½ in. Fist: 13½ in.
Career span: 1957–1973
Record: 54 fights, 45 wins (21 KOs), 9 losses (no KOs)
Age at which title was won: 25, in his 41st fight

Championship defences
25.5.65 Ali w.KO.1 Sonny Liston (USA) at Lewiston, Maine
 1.11.65 Terrell w.pts.15 George Chuvalo (CAN) at Toronto
22.11.65 Ali w.rsf.12 Floyd Patterson (USA) at Las Vegas
29.3.66 Ali w.pts.12 George Chuvalo (Can) at Toronto
21.5.66 Ali w.rsf.6 Henry Cooper (GB) at Highbury
28.6.66 Terrell w.pts.15 Doug Jones (USA) at Houston
 6.8.66 Ali w.KO.3 Brian London (GB) at Earls Court
10.9.66 Ali w.rsf.12 Karl Mildenberger (GER) at Frankfurt
14.11.66 Ali w.rsf.3 Cleveland Williams (USA) at Houston
 6.2.67 Ali w.pts. 15 Ernie Terrell (USA) at Houston
(Ali recognized as undisputed champion)
22.3.67 Ali w.KO.7 Zora Folley (USA) at New York

(Ali was stripped of the title for refusing to join the US army. Joe Frazier stopped Buster Mathis in 11 rounds for the New York version of the vacant title on 4 March 1968, at New York. Jimmy Ellis outpointed Jerry Quarry for the WBA version of the title on 27 April 1968, at Oakland.)

Joe Frazier

Born Beaufort, South Carolina, 12 January 1944
Ht.: 5 ft. 11½ in. Wt.: 14 st. 7 lb.
Reach: 73½ in. Chest: 42–44 in. Fist: 13 in.
Nickname: Smokin' Joe
Olympic heavyweight champion 1964
Career span: 1965–1976
Record: 36 fights, 32 wins (27 KOs), 4 losses (KO'd 3)
Age at which title was won: 24, in his 20th fight

Jimmy Ellis

Born Louisville, Kentucky, 24 February 1940
Ht.: 6 ft. 1 in. Wt.: 14 st. 4 lb.
Reach: 76 in. Chest: 42–44½ in. Fist: 12¾ in.
Nickname: The Cobra
Career span: 1961–1975
Record: 53 fights, 40 wins, 1 draw, 12 losses (KO'd 4)
Age at which title was won: 28, in his 31st fight

Championship defences
24.6.68   Frazier w.ret.2 Manuel Ramos (MEX) at New York
14.9.68   Ellis w.pts.15 Floyd Patterson (USA) at Stockholm
10.12.68 Frazier w.pts.15 Oscar Bonavena (ARG) at Philadelphia
22.4.69   Frazier w.KO.1 Dave Zyglewicz (USA) at Houston
23.6.69   Frazier w.rsf.7 Jerry Quarry (USA) at New York
16.2.70   Frazier w.ret.4 Jimmy Ellis (USA) at New York

(Frazier recognized as undisputed champion)
18.11.70 Frazier w.KO.2 Bob Foster (USA) at Detroit
 8.3.71   Frazier w.pts.15 Muhammad Ali (USA) at New York
15.1.72   Frazier w.rsf.4 Terry Daniels (USA) at New Orleans
25.5.72   Frazier w.rsf.4 Ron Stander (USA) at Omaha
22.1.73   Frazier l.rsf.2 George Foreman (USA) at Kingston, Jamaica

George Foreman

Born Marshall, Texas, 10 January 1948
Ht.: 6 ft. 3½ in. Wt.: 15 st. 12 lb.
Reach: 82 in. Chest: 42–44½ in. Fist: 12 in.
Olympic heavyweight champion 1968
Career span: 1969–1977
Record: 47 fights, 45 wins (42 KOs), 2 losses (KO'd 1)
Age at which title was won: 25, in his 38th fight

Championship defences
 1.9.73   w.KO.1 Joe Roman (USA) at Tokyo
26.3.74   w.rsf.2 Ken Norton (USA) at Caracas
30.10.74 l.KO.8 Muhammad Ali (USA) at Zaire
(Ali regained the championship)
24.3.75   Ali w.rsf.15 Chuck Wepner (USA) at Cleveland
16.5.75   Ali w.rsf.11 Ron Lyle (USA) at Las Vegas
 1.7.75   Ali w.pts.15 Joe Bugner (GB) at Kuala Lumpur
 1.10.75 Ali w.ret.14 Joe Frazier (USA) at Manila
10.2.75   Ali w.KO.5 Jean-Pierre Coopman (BEL) at San Juan, Puerto Rico
30.4.76   Ali w.pts.15 Jimmy Young (USA) at Landover, Maryland
25.5.76   Ali w.rsf.5 Richard Dunn (GB) at Munich
28.9.76   Ali w.pts.15 Ken Norton (USA) at New York
16.5.77   Ali w.pts.15 Alfredo Evangelista (URU) at Landover, Maryland

29.9.77   Ali w.pts.15 Earnie Shavers (USA) at New York
15.2.78   Ali l.pts.15 Leon Spinks (USA) at Las Vegas

Leon Spinks

Born St Louis, 11 July 1953
Ht.: 6 ft. 2 in. Wt.: 14 st.
Reach: 76 in. Chest: 40½–42 in. Fist: 12½ in.
Olympic light-heavyweight champion 1976
Career span: 1977–
Record: 19 fights, 13 wins (8 KOs), 2 draws, 4 losses (no KOs)
Age at which title was won: 24, in his 8th fight

(Spinks was stripped of the title by the WBC for his failure to
defend against Ken Norton, who was named as their new champion
following his 'final eliminator' points victory over Jimmy Young on
5 November 1977, in Las Vegas.)

Ken Norton

Born Jacksonville, Illinois, 9 August 1945
Ht.: 6 ft. 3 in. Wt.: 15 st. 6 lb.
Reach: 80 in. Chest: 45–48. in. Fist: 13 in.
Career span: 1967–1981
Record: 50 fights, 42 wins (3 KOs), 1 draw, 7 losses (KO'd 4)
Age at which the title was won: 32, in his 44th fight

Championship defence
10.6.78   l.pts.15 Larry Holmes (USA) at Las Vegas

Larry Holmes

Born Cuthbert, Georgia, 3 November 1949
Ht.: 6 ft. 4 in. Wt.: 15 st. 2 lb.
Reach: 81 in. Chest: 45–48 in. Fist: 13½ in.
Nickname: Black Cloud
Career span: 1973–1985
Record: 48 fights, 48 wins (34 KOs)
Retired as undefeated champion
Age at which title was won: 28, in his 28th fight

Championship defences:
15.9.78   Muhammad Ali w.pts.15 Leon Spinks at New Orleans
(Ali regained the title for a second time)

10.11.78 Holmes w.KO.7 Alfredo Evangelista (URU) at Las Vegas
24.3.79 Holmes w.rsf.7 Osvaldo Ocasio (Puerto Rico) at Las Vegas
22.6.79 Holmes w.rsf.12 Mike Weaver (USA) at New York
28.9.79 Holmes w.rsf.11 Earnie Shavers (USA) at Las Vegas

(Ali announced his retirement as WBA champion. John Tate outpointed South African Gerrie Coetzee for the vacant WBA title on 20 October 1979, at Pretoria.

John Tate

Born Knoxville, Tennessee, 29 January 1955
Ht.: 6 ft. 4 in. Wt.: 17 st.
Reach: 78 in. Chest: 42–44 in. Fist: 13 in.
Career span: 1977–
Record: 32 fights, 30 wins (21 KOs), 2 losses
Age at which title was won: 24, in his 20th fight

Championship defences
 3.2.80 Holmes w.ko.6 Lorenzo Zanon (ITA) at Las Vegas
31.3.80 Holmes w.pts.15 Trevor Berbick (CAN) at Las Vegas
31.3.80 Tate l.KO.15 Mike Weaver (USA) at Knoxville

Mike Weaver

Born Gatesville, Texas, 14 June 1952
Ht.: 6 ft. 1 in. Wt.: 14 st. 8 lb.
Reach: 78½ in. Chest: 44½–46½ in. Fist: 13½ in.
Career span: 1972–
Record: 36 fights, 25 wins (16 KOs), 1 draw, 10 losses (KO'd 6)
Age at which title was won: 27, in his 30th contest

Championship defences
 7.7.80 Holmes w.rsf.7 Scott LeDoux (USA) at Bloomington
 2.10.80 Holmes w.ret.10 Muhammad Ali (USA) at Las Vegas
25.10.80 Weaver w.KO.13 Gerrie Coetzee (SA) at Sun City
11.4.81 Holmes w.pts.15 Trevor Berbick (CAN) at Las Vegas
12.6.81 Holmes w.rsf.3 Leon Spinks (USA) at Detroit
 3.10.81 Weaver w.pts.15 James Tillis (USA) at Rosemount
 6.11.81 Holmes w.rsf.11 Renaldo Snipes (USA) at Pittsburgh
11.6.82 Holmes w.dis.13 Gerry Cooney (USA) at Las Vegas
26.11.82 Holmes w.pts.15 Randy Cobb (USA) at Houston
10.12.82 Weaver l.rsf.1 Mike Dokes at Las Vegas